EQUINE

ER

EQUINE
ER

Stories from a Year in the Life of an Equine Veterinary Hospital

LESLIE GUTTMAN

LEXINGTON, KENTUCKY

Library of Congress Control Number: 2009922184

ISBN 978-1-58150-213-8

Printed in the United States
First Edition: 2009

a division of
Blood-Horse Publications
PUBLISHERS SINCE 1916

Contents

Note to the Reader

Equine ER is a work of nonfiction, meaning all the events are true. Medical cases and other events were either witnessed as they happened, or reconstructed from multiple interviews and materials such as medical charts, newspaper accounts, and video. Some clients of Rood & Riddle Equine Hospital asked for anonymity, and some horses' names have been changed. In one chapter, Hello Weekend, a handful of identifying details of horses and their owners have been changed. I am grateful to the equine health care magazine *The Horse*, whose medical coverage was invaluable to the research and fact-checking of this book.

Prologue: Derby Day

The three-month-old filly had been fine the day before, running around, frisky; she was chestnut, a daub of white on her forehead. But today, she couldn't get up. She was a big foal, architecturally perfect, the daughter of a dam and sire (mother and father) descended from Thoroughbred royalty; her bloodlines stretched back to Northern Dancer, one of the most influential sires of modern times. Her features were delicate and ethereal, a fairy-tale foal. The owner thought she was the most beautiful foal he'd ever seen, and he's seen quite a few. He and his wife breed and race Thoroughbreds, and are both so horse-crazy they named their own daughters after famous racehorses.

The filly, whom I will call Girlchild, had been found that morning by the manager of the Bluegrass farm where she was boarded, in the paddock near her mother. The foal was lying down and could not rise. The grass around her was flattened, as if she had been struggling to get up. Usually, sleeping or resting foals jump up and dart off when you get close to them, but Girlchild lay still when the farm manager approached her. When the manager waved her hand in front of the foal's eyes, Girlchild didn't blink; it was as if she wasn't all there. The foal was the liveliest of that year's crop, the playful favorite of the farm manager, who knew something was seriously wrong and had her taken immediately to Rood & Riddle Equine Hospital in Lexington. Vets took X-rays of Girlchild's spine, but the radiographs didn't show any damage. X-rays, however, aren't foolproof, so the foal was knocked out and placed on her back in the clinic's MRI. All you could see was the lower half of her body sticking out from under the dome of the scanner. Her haunches were splayed. An intern monitored her depth of anesthesia, as well as her ventilation, heart rate, blood pressure, and other vital signs in the dim room dominated by the giant white magnet. Dr. Peter Morresey stared at the foal from the adjacent monitoring room through the glass window. Morresey had taken over the case for Dr. Bryan Waldridge, who had been kicked by a mare in his right calf that morning. Waldridge was currently being seen at a nearby hospital, where he wished the doctor would show him the radiographs of his leg right away as he did for the owners of the horses he X-rayed; Waldridge wanted to get back to work. Large-animal vets aren't known for being able to sit still for long.

It was the day of the 2008 Kentucky Derby, the first Saturday in May. For horse people everywhere, but especially in the Bluegrass, Derby Day is a religious holiday. Thousands of people were preparing to watch the race at Churchill Downs or on TV, and between taking care of patients some Rood & Riddle staff members would be able to catch the race in the admissions office. Although they didn't know it yet, those staff members would see the death of Eight Belles, the charcoal-gray filly who would break down after finishing second and be euthanized immediately because of the depth of her injuries. Her shocking death on national television would bring significant changes to the racing world, with equine vets such as

Rood & Riddle's Dr. Larry Bramlage playing key roles in the debate and discussion the filly's death ignited.

This book is about the year I spent starting in spring 2008 following around the veterinarians at Rood & Riddle, one of the most prominent equine hospitals in the country. It is about these veterinarians' world and the horse-smitten clients and four-footed patients within it. Hospitals are places where life turns on a dime, and this one is no different: I saw lives saved, lost, and remade. I also saw that alongside the advanced veterinary medicine being performed exists something timeless about the job of an equine veterinarian ... found in experiences such as the small miracle of watching a foal, slick from the birth canal, get up and walk for the first time, wobbly but persevering. Or in the ritual of an equine vet making a farm call in spring, his or her truck rattling up to an old black barn, past paddocks colored kelly green from the rain and dotted with mares and foals.

Rood & Riddle Equine Hospital sits on twenty-four acres of what used to be part of the old Nursery Stud farm, where Man o' War was born on a spring day in 1917. The grounds are lush, with plantings such as lilac and forsythia bushes, azaleas and Russian sage, and white pines, red oaks, magnolias, and spruce trees. The practice has more than fifty vets and a staff of over 200 people: nursing techs, farriers, barn crew, business staff, administrative assistants, and more. Nineteen of the veterinarians are ambulatory, meaning they are out in the field visiting farms all day, in trucks packed tight with all the medications and supplies they'll need, including snacks like salted almonds and Girl Scout cookies since they rarely have time to stop to eat. On the property are nine barns with 140 stalls. Two of them are isolation barns for infectious diseases such as Salmonella. The hospital's buildings include a surgery unit, a podiatry center, a reproductive center, its own pharmacy, and lab. The property is rectangular, and the barns and business offices sit at precise angles to each other. It feels, as surgeon Rolf Embertson puts it, much like a campus. The buildings are chocolate brown split-face concrete block, with tongue-and-groove vaulted ceilings in many of the barns. The grounds are noticeable for what you don't see: horse droppings. Whatever is pooped is immediately scooped by the first person to witness the event; it is almost like it never happens.

Much like Hewlett Packard and Apple Computer, also started in their garages by their founders, Rood & Riddle has come a long way from Dr. Bill Rood's one-man show in his garage, the hospital's origins in 1980. The staff then consisted of one retired neighbor stocking the pharmacy and a former waitress Rood had hired away from a Mexican restaurant to be its only tech. Rood first met Dr. Tom Riddle in 1981; both men were looking for another equine veterinarian with whom to form a partnership. They teamed up the following year and opened the hospital in its current location in 1986. It was about a quarter of the size it is now.

At that time, there was already a big, established equine veterinary practice in town, Hagyard-Davidson-McGee Associates (now called Hagyard Equine Medical Institute). Founded in 1876, it was, and is, known for taking care of greats like Man o' War and Secretariat, as well as horses Queen Elizabeth II once boarded in Lexington at Darby Dan Farm. But Rood and Riddle were relatively young and ambitious, thirty-eight and thirty-four, and already used to working endless hours; neither wanted to work those kinds of hours for anybody else. Because of their youth, they were also too foolish and untested by life, as Riddle says, to worry about failure. Today, meeting Rood, the personable mellow-voiced hospital director in his sixties, a heartbreaker in his day, it's not hard to imagine him as a young, brash entrepreneur going up against Hagyard's, as everyone calls it. It's harder to imagine the quieter Riddle as a risk-taker, a man

Rood & Riddle has come a long way since its origins in a garage.

In the early days, Tom Riddle and Bill Rood had debt and determination.

who almost talked himself out of seeing his own filly run in (and win) a race at Churchill Downs on Derby Day because he thought he shouldn't take a day off work during foaling season. But underneath their seemingly different exteriors — Rood, the laid-back easy-come, easy-goer, and Riddle, the self-described reader of the fine print — they are alike in that both want a big say in their own fates, and are willing to take the chances to have it.

The two went $1.8 million in debt to start the hospital (they had $1,000 between them in cash). The bank chief father of a college friend of Rood's paved the way for the loans. When they sent out invitations to the hospital's open house, a prominent equine veterinarian in town was heard to say, "I won't be there for the open house, but I'll come to the bankruptcy auction." That veterinarian underestimated the impact of his statement on the two men, and the fuel that has driven so many entrepreneurs to succeed: pride. Rood and Riddle wanted to stay in Lexington; the horse world is insular; and they were determined not to implode inside it with everyone looking on.

That determination paid off. Since then, some of the most well-known Thoroughbreds in the world have been through the hospital, such as the last two to win the Triple Crown, Seattle Slew and Affirmed. But along with the Thoroughbred athletes, many other kinds of horses are treated, from miniature ponies kept as pasture pets to Clydesdales that pull wedding carriages, and the occasional llama. Today, the practice is a multi-million dollar partnership. One of the partners has his own string of polo ponies. But these veterinarians work hard, crazy-hard, for their money, and sacrifice many hours of personal and family time. I'm still trying to figure out when they

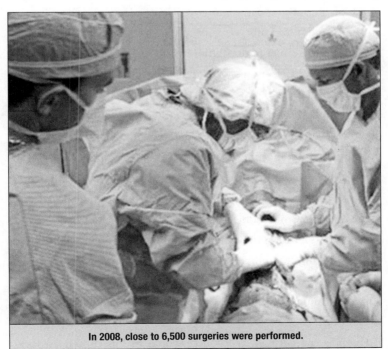

In 2008, close to 6,500 surgeries were performed.

sleep. Or eat. Rood told me that at the first partners retreat about twelve years ago, in a rare private conversation among the veterinarians (all men at the time) about the costs of their profession, some wept when talking about the time they had missed with their kids, and the pressure on their intimate relationships from the weight of the work.

The demands of their work ultimately stem from the sheer number of cases they treat. Approximately 11,000 horses come into the clinic each year, and ambulatory vets attend to roughly another 5,000. In 2008, close to 6,500 surgeries were performed. (However, in 2009 the economy had affected the clinic. The caseload was expected to be down approximately 5 percent by year's end, and some part-time employees were laid off.)

With all the cases come some knotty situations. Riddle is an admirer of the late veterinarian-writer James Herriot, whose stories have inspired numerous young people to go to veterinary school, including interns I met at the clinic. Herriot once said, "If only vetting just consisted of treating sick animals. But it didn't. There were so many other things."

At Rood & Riddle, some of those other things are client-related dilemmas in emergencies. Owners can be difficult to reach, living or traveling in different time zones, even different hemispheres. Sometimes a farm manager or barn crew member will bring a horse in, and then give the go-ahead if the animal needs immediate surgery. Later, the owner might object to the cost and the fact he or she wasn't consulted first. Vets at times have to watch animals suffer while owners are making the difficult decisions about whether to do surgery or euthanize, or while insurance agents have their own vets do required examinations. Just as with regular doctors, the paperwork is voluminous.

The bills can get high at Rood & Riddle, numbering in the thousands of dollars. Clients are paying not just for the veterinarians' knowledge and skill at one of the most elite equine hospitals in the world, they are also paying for the *care*. Take the ICU and neonate unit, for example, full of Thoroughbred foals and mares starting in January through June (foaling season). The foals sleep on comfy Tempur-pedic mattresses made for people, with fleece blankets, electric blankets, and other bedding. Tasks for each patient are performed at fifteen-minute, one-hour, and two-hour intervals. Vital signs are taken, medications checked, sheets changed. Patients get physical therapy; they're turned to avoid bed sores or in the case of a foal whose ribs aren't fractured, propped up to keep trying out their new legs and learn to nurse. Some foals can't blink yet so ointment is continually rubbed on their eyes to mimic tear film. Foals can be on

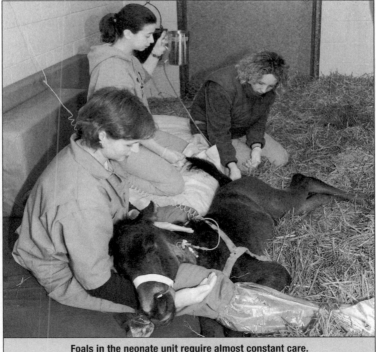

Foals in the neonate unit require almost constant care.

five different IV fluids simultaneously, and the pumps are the same type as those used in human hospitals. The biosecurity in the unit, and in the hospital as a whole, is strict to prevent infection, cross-contamination, and zoonotic diseases (animal-to-human transmission). Many of the medications are ones civilians would recognize: Valium, dopamine, and morphine, for example, along with broad-spectrum antibiotics.

Most non-horse people don't know that for all their grace, horses are stupendously accident-prone. They get hurt running into fences, running into each other, running into trees, getting stuck under fences and panicking, trying to jump fences and not quite making it, getting struck by lightning (really), getting their legs stuck in groundhog holes, wrenching their necks, kicking each other, stepping on each other ... and so on. Numerous patients come in to Rood & Riddle without their owners knowing what led to their problems, as was the case with Girlchild, the foal in the MRI on

Dr. Peter Morresey examines a sick foal.

Derby Day. She had no signs of injury, but that wasn't unusual; she could have hidden swelling. A horse cannot tell its doctor what happened or where it hurts or feels numb. Their illnesses are very often mysteries.

Back in the monitoring room opposite the MRI, Dr. Peter Morresey continued to stare at Girlchild through the glass while Dr. Katie Garrett sat in front of a computer screen looking at the images of the foal's brain and cervical spine. The regions being assessed were the most likely places of injury, corresponding to the fact that the foal was unable to use all four legs.

Morresey initially thought Girlchild had gotten up the wrong way and wrenched her neck. But now he actually believed she had been running, tripped, and fallen flat on her face and forehead so hard that her head then snapped back, causing trauma to the junction of the brain and spinal cord. She had some loose teeth, which helped lead to his theory.

Morresey is from New Zealand, where he also attended vet school. He is in his early forties, medium-height, reddish-brown hair, blue eyes, and a penchant for saying "Rocktacular," when he's pleased. He talks very, very fast. He doesn't drink coffee, and I don't think he needs it.

In the monitoring room, Garrett pointed at a spot on the screen. It was the joint where the skull and the first cervical vertebra meet, the atlanto-occipital junction. "Yes," she said, "it looks irregular here."

Morresey looked down and pointed at another small area on the image. "What's that black thing?"

"It could be fibrous tissue … a V.D. (ventral dorsal) radiograph is going to give us a better global view in any case," she replied.

"Get me some horizontal action," said Morresey, and Garrett clicked so the image on the screen rotated from vertical. The black, white, and gray slices of the brain and spine undulated in and out of focus as Garrett paged up and down.

"For this foal not to be able to get up," she said, "it should have something more prominent."

"I was expecting to see some cervical cord swelling," said Morresey.

Garrett clicked on the image and enlarged it. "Look, it's not ear-shaped," she said, pointing at the left side of the junction, which did not match the right. "But we're not perfectly transverse (meaning the images weren't being taken perpendicular to the axis of the spinal column). We're almost duty-bound to (spinal) tap it." She couldn't tell if the asymmetry was actually in the atlanto-occipital region, or if the image was off because the foal's neck was slightly bent. It's almost impossible to get a horse's entire neck perfectly aligned in the bore of the magnet.

Morresey got a call on his Blackberry and went to the next room to take it. The MRI took its last seven-minute scan, making its loud *booong, booong, booong* noise.

In the next room, Morresey answered a call from an equine insurance agent. She was at the Derby and had to yell into the phone to be heard over the crowd. She was asking about another foal case. "I had to euthanize that foal," Morresey said. "It was arresting ... neurologically, this foal was no longer with us ... its heart kept stopping ... it wasn't associated with its environment, profuse diarrhea, Salmonella, the foal was in a bad position, and it couldn't get around to heal itself. Yes. Once the foal lost its pupillary light response ... I'm sorry you were called after the event. The paperwork's been done, and it's going around the corner for a necropsy. OK." He listened for a few seconds. "OK," he said, "sounds good."

Morresey returned as the scan finished. After a few moments, he, Garrett, and two interns took the foal out of the magnet and into the recovery area. The intern who had been monitoring the foal under anesthesia continued to do so in recovery while the second intern prepared to do a spinal tap. With the foal on her right side, head flexed down, the intern lined up the needle and made several unsuccessful attempts to do the tap. The procedure is tricky; you have to put the needle into the space between the back of the skull and the first cervical vertebra (a space about the size of a quarter) at the correct angle to collect the spinal fluid. If you go too far, you can hit the spinal cord and exacerbate existing problems or create serious new ones. What makes it even trickier is that a foal's anatomy is so much smaller than that of a grown horse.

Morresey, opposite the intern, flexed the foal's head down a bit more to open up the space. "Now, you'll feel a distinct pop … " he said. "Move slightly forward. That's pretty good, like that. Just make sure you're right this way." The intern still couldn't get it.

Morresey took over and did the tap. The fluid that came out was bloody.

"Do you think I made that?" the intern said worriedly, "I don't think I was ever in there."

"No," Morresey replied, "It makes a pop when you go in there. Did you feel it?"

"No," she said.

Morresey asked her to nod the slumbering foal's head up and down from the sides as he held it at the top, feeling for fractures or bony abnormality. "It's separating," he said, of the atlanto-occipital junction. "It's almost like a sandpaper feel." He was feeling bony fragments rubbing against each other, indicative of damage. Usually the joint would be smooth going back and forth, like when you flex your wrist. With the rough joint and the bloody tap, he thought out loud that there had definitely been trauma to the back of the brain.

"That would fit with the MRI," said Garrett, looking on. The situation was worrisome for the foal, the vets thought. Morresey would

keep her on anti-inflammatories and other medications to both reduce swelling in the central nervous tissue and the pain that might
cause the foal to thrash around and further injure herself. But it
wasn't clear at this point if she would ever walk again.

Earlier, Garrett had driven the gator, a green-and-yellow mini
all-terrain vehicle, down to the MRI building. Now, she opened the
doors to the recovery room and pulled over a large green hard-plastic
stretcher, known as the glide, from the side of the room. It looked
almost like a sled. Then she, Morresey, and the two interns used an
electric hoist to get the foal off the table and onto the glide. Garrett put a small, blue hard-foam pillow under the foal's head and
hooked the glide to the vehicle. With one of the interns sitting on the
stretcher holding the foal in place, Garrett drove slowly up to Barn
3, dragging the intern and horse behind her, with the other two vets
following on foot like bodyguards.

Girlchild's dam was a good-sized dark bay. She paced around the
stall like a mom whose child had gone missing at the mall. The vets
moved the foal off the stretcher into the stall, and then carefully spin-
rolled her onto a straw bed. The mother stood over the foal, never
taking her eyes off her.

While the vets finished up with Girlchild, the Kentucky Derby was
getting ready to start, and up at the admissions office some of the
hospital staff had crowded around the wide-screen TV to watch the
race. The screen flashed Bernie Stutts, the seventy-year-old Florida
trainer who, after forty years in the business, was running a horse in
the Derby for the first time. Then came a shot of Eight Belles, "the
first filly in twenty years!" the announcer said.

It was a windy day at Churchill. The co-anchor held onto her wide-
brimmed black hat as she started the final round of pre-race reporting. The horses began their path to the starting gate, accompanied
by lead ponies with flowers in their tails. The camera panned the fa-

vorites: Colonel John, Big Brown, Pyro. As he came out of the tunnel, jockey E.T. Baird was bucked off Recapturetheglory, and everyone in the admissions office laughed knowingly. Numerous employees at Rood & Riddle had their own horses.

On television, the bugle sang, the horses loaded, and the Derby began. Bob Black Jack, a longshot, took the lead. At the far turn, Big Brown made his move. For a breath, it looked like Eight Belles was going to catch him. Then the unbeaten bay, ridden by Cajun jockey Kent Desormeaux, dubbed "The Kid" in his days as a teen phenomenon, pulled away. Desormeaux galloped home on the horse like he stole him. Everyone cheered. A few seconds later, there was a gasp as the TV flashed on a collapsed horse. It was Eight Belles.

The newscasters struggled with the unscripted event. Everyone in the admissions office waited for more information, while the screen showed trainer Rick Dutrow celebrating, unaware of what had happened down at the track.

Dr. Larry Bramlage faced the cameras at Churchill Downs.

Then the camera flashed to an anchor standing next to Rood & Riddle veterinarian Larry Bramlage, past president of the American Association of Equine Practitioners and an on-call vet and commentator for the Derby. Although Bramlage was supposed to give an update, he had just gotten a call and was on his cell phone. It was awkward for the anchor who fumbled with what to say to the TV audience. The call was from Dr. Scott Hopper, another veterinarian at Rood & Riddle who was also working on-call for the AAEP. Hopper was down at the track by Eight Belles. He gave Bramlage the news about the filly, who had just been put down.

The camera flashed away and in a few moments returned to Bramlage, off his cell. He looked as if he was trying to compose himself. "She broke both front ankles," he said of Eight Belles. "They had to euthanize immediately." (With her fractures, bones had come through the skin, creating a deadly entryway for infection that made her impossible to save.)

Everyone in the admissions office was silent.

Eight Belles was the first Thoroughbred ever to die in the 134-year history of the Kentucky Derby. Her death would mark the beginning of months of pressure on racing to re-evaluate how it does things. That pressure continues today. The issues under examination range from the use of dirt tracks and steroids to whether market forces have gone too far in shaping how horses are bred, creating a fast, light Thoroughbred that runs fewer races for bigger purses (and then moves on quickly to the breeding shed) rather than a horse designed for soundness, longevity, and the athleticism and tradition of the sport itself. Numerous owners, trainers, breeders, and racing fans would begin a period of difficult introspection that also continues.

But right now in the hospital admissions office, it was just disbelief over Eight Belles. After about ten minutes, most of the staff had to get back to work, but a handful stayed and tried to wrap their heads around what had happened. One of them was a young woman on the barn crew, her light brown hair under a baseball cap. "Talk about running your heart out," she said.

Morresey had missed the Derby. He was too busy trying to figure out the Girlchild enigma. He was going to give the foal cold intravenous fluids as was done the year before for Kevin Everett, the Buffalo Bills football player who had severely injured his spinal cord on the field. The theory is that the fluids may reduce inflammation and potential hemorrhage. Everett (who also had surgery and extensive rehabilitation) can now, almost miraculously, walk again.

In Barn 3, Girlchild had woken up and was sitting quietly on her straw bed, fuzzy and alert, an intelligent look in her eyes. She looked sweet, as cute as a wild strawberry. Later that night, she had a seizure and died.

For her owner, "it was completely devastating." It wasn't by any means his first loss or unexpected accident, but he never gets used to it. When they had found the foal on the ground that morning, he'd known there probably wasn't much that could be done, but he had still held out hope that she might recover. He told me he'd have to make himself get over it: "You have to move on in this business, or you have to get out of this business."

Morresey hadn't thought Girlchild had a good chance of recovering. But he knew it was better for any horse to die quickly, by fate's plan or by euthanasia, than for suffering to drag on. During the year I spent at Rood & Riddle, I learned that so many things can go wrong with a horse, especially a racehorse, from fetus to foal, weanling to yearling to adulthood. (Once I asked Riddle if writer E.B. White's advice to anyone moving to New York to pursue his or her dreams also applies to raising a Thoroughbred. Riddle said yes. The advice: No one should try it unless they are willing to be lucky.)

But I also saw that breathtaking comebacks occur just as often as the losses. A horse's desire to live is just as important as it is with a human patient. What I saw is that, like at the racetrack, the odds don't determine the outcome. Nothing is impossible, and anything can happen.

Hello Weekend

Twenty-four hours spent at the hospital

It was Friday night. 10 p.m. Late February. Across Lexington, the workweek behind them, regular people were out enjoying themselves, or tucked in at home, but none of the veterinarians at Rood & Riddle had any such plans. Every year, from roughly February through June, the vets are slammed with patients day and night. In addition to the usual emergencies — fractures, lacerations, other traumas — it is foaling season: Mares can have problematic births (called dystocias), usually because foals are in the wrong position — instead of feet and head first, they can be sideways, upside-down, their heads tucked between their legs as if they can't face leaving the womb. Once out, foals can have contracted legs, neurological issues, gut problems. Sometimes a mare hemorrhages or dies from the strain of giving birth. Mares often experience colic post-foaling as well, and the spring season brings more colicking for all horses because of changes in weather and because as horses begin feeding on new grass, their often-delicate digestive systems react. (Colic refers to pain caused by the intestinal tract being blocked, bloated, or

(In some cases, identifying details of owners and horses have been changed.)

irritated for a variety of reasons.) Up at admissions, an emergency colic case had just arrived.

The patient, a smoke-colored mare, was led into a padded stall where she collapsed on her side, moaning. Several interns attended to the horse as her owner watched anxiously. A few moments passed, and then the mare's diaphragm was still. "Is she breathing?" someone asked. Dr. Sarah Gray pressed her knee into the horse's chest; the stimulation got the mare to take a breath. Dr. Alexandra Tracey listened to her heartbeat. It was erratic.

All of a sudden, the horse jumped to her feet and barreled toward the interns, who darted out of the room and shut the heavy door to keep from getting trampled. Then the mare collapsed again. The interns went back in. (Horses in severe colic will often collapse from the abdominal pain.)

Dr. Rolf Embertson, one of the hospital's surgeons, appeared. It was his weekend on call. Even the top veterinarians at the hospital work 24/7 in foaling season. One of the interns told him she'd given the mare 150 mg of xylazine, a drug for sedation. "What are her membranes like?" Embertson asked her. He was referring to the mucous membranes visible on a horse's gums, the color of which can be a barometer for how efficiently the heart is pumping and oxygenated blood is circulating throughout the body.

The membranes were pale pink when the mare was up, within the bubblegum palette of normalcy, but a purplish color when she was down. It is unusual for the color to change. The purplish color might signify that she wasn't oxygenating her blood well when down. She could also be heading into septicemia, a potentially deadly condition where bacteria or bacterial toxins invade the bloodstream, in this case most likely wrought by a strangulated bowel.

The horse moaned again. The owner flinched. She told Embertson, "She started (colicking) at five (p.m.)," and added she'd also

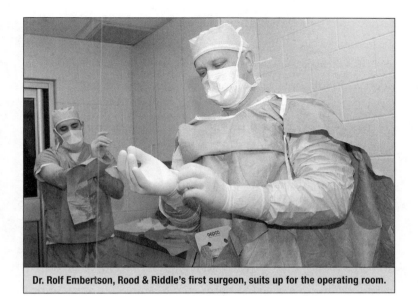

Dr. Rolf Embertson, Rood & Riddle's first surgeon, suits up for the operating room.

given the horse substantial pain medication herself. The mare was a twenty-one-year-old pasture pet who had always been prone to colic, sensitive to everything from changes in weather to deworming, but the owner had never seen her like this. Her colics had always resolved on their own.

The horse rose again quickly. Gray's hand got smacked against the wall. Then the mare collapsed and tried to roll, but there wasn't enough room. "You can't roll in here, baby," said Brent Comer, a nursing staff supervisor and tech who had arrived to help out. Then the mare got to her feet again.

"Keep her walking," said Embertson. He also told the interns to give her more xylazine and perform an ultrasound exam of the abdomen.

Embertson was calm as he discussed the situation with the owner, telling her that they were going through standard diagnostic procedures to try and figure out the origin of the mare's colic. Embertson is always even, stoic, contained. Californians would say he has good boundaries. He is in his early fifties, tall, trim, one of those men who although he has lost all his hair, wears his dome well, like a professional athlete. He was the first surgeon hired at Rood & Riddle over twenty years ago and has been instrumental in the hospital's growth and success. Someone once described his personality to me as like that of a Quarter Horse, one of the hardest-working and most versatile breeds: Whatever needs to be done, no matter how much, he can do it.

Back with the owner, Embertson explained the mare might need surgery.

"I don't want to put her through that torture," she replied.

"Let's see if we can figure out a little more what's wrong with her," Embertson said, adding that he wanted to do a rectal palpation.

But first Tracey needed to finish an ultrasound. As she scanned the beige probe across the mare's abdomen, she saw the large colon had quite a bit of gas in it. But that was all the intern could see.

The owner was distraught. She was embarrassed by her emotions and explained to Embertson how much she loved the horse. He told her he understood. He and his wife were having a birthday party on Sunday for one of their ten horses; the mare was turning thirty.

Embertson began palpating the mare. He could feel the large colon was displaced (out of its normal position), but it was impossible to tell how severely and whether part of it was twisted, shutting off blood flow. While he palpated, Dr. Albert Solé Guitart quickly collected peritoneal fluid — liquid from the abdominal cavity. If there had been a gastrointestinal rupture, the fluid would show elevated protein and white blood cell levels, and, usually, bacteria and plant material.

Then the vets refluxed the mare (obtaining stomach contents via a tube, threaded through the nasal passage). They didn't find an excessive amount of drained liquid, signifying the mare's problem likely originated in the gastrointestinal tract. The results from her bloodwork and peritoneal fluid came back normal, meaning, at least for now, she didn't have a rupture.

Embertson told the owner about the displacement. From the amount of pain, it was also likely the mare had a twist in the large colon. The options at that moment were: surgery; waiting to see if the colic would resolve on its own with the clinic's help (providing fluids, pain meds, and laxatives); or euthanization. But those options were more complicated than they sounded. Surgery entailed cost, perhaps more than she might want to spend. The average cost for a colic surgery ranges between $4,500 and $6,000. Even though the hospital does successful surgeries for large colon displacements all the time, the cost could go up if they ran into unexpected problems on the table, or if the mare didn't recover well. If they waited to see if the situation would resolve, then the issues were 1) how long could they manage her pain, and 2) if they eventually did decide to do surgery, then they would have likely put the mare through significant pain for nothing. Also, waiting too long to operate could create more, possibly fatal, problems such as a rupture. Euthanization, of course, meant no turning back.

Embertson thought it unlikely the mare's colic would resolve on its own. Regardless of all the tests, he told her, "I go on pain." The pain's severity and duration in the face of medication was often the most important factor in deciding whether to go to surgery, he explained. "She's got 300 milligrams of Rompun (the brand name for xylazine) in her," but was still struggling.

In the stall, the mare collapsed again.

The owner was having trouble comprehending that she had to make an irreversible decision fairly quickly. It was hard to take it all in.

"Sometimes the least expensive thing is to go to surgery," Embertson said. "If we wait, then put her through all that pain, and then decide, the bill is even higher."

Another hour passed; Embertson needed to know how to proceed. The horse wasn't improving, her pain increasing. Surgery now looked like the best option to save her.

But the owner still worried about hurting the mare by putting her on the operating table.

"The biggest question is: Is it something we can fix?" Embertson replied. "If it's something we can fix (like a large colon displacement), we should go to surgery. If it's a pain issue, it's not inhumane to go to surgery; it's inhumane for your pocketbook. That's just the truth. ... If it's pain you're worried about, the way to get rid of the pain is surgery."

In the background you could hear the interns slapping the horse's side, trying to get her to stand up.

The owner looked down. "If we decide to do surgery, how soon can you do it?"

"Now," Embertson said.

The owner still couldn't give him an answer. Embertson checked on the mare again; she was breaking through the pain medication every ten minutes. The interns thought the pain was now unbearable. The vet returned. The owner told him the horse had had a good life. Embertson said he empathized; he had a dog at home he also faced putting down. Silence followed.

"How do you do it?" she asked.

"We sedate her heavily and then give her an injection," said Embertson. More silence. Then the owner said she wanted to euthanize. She didn't give a reason. Likely it was a combination of knowing the mare had had a long life plus the cost of the surgery.

The owner wept on the horse's mane, saying good-bye. Then

the mare started to shift and moan. The drugs were wearing off again.

The owner left the room. One of the interns injected the mare. Her chest rose and fell, and then stopped. Life left the room; you could feel it.

Embertson watched. He hadn't wanted to put her down. He started to second-guess his conversations with the owner. "I could have pushed harder to go to surgery," he said to me. "We could have saved her." Then he told Comer to make sure to listen to the mare's heart before they took the body away.

"I will," Comer said, as he braided a section of the horse's mane and cut it off for the owner while Tracey did the same with the tail. I asked Comer if they always did that.

"Yes," he said, "or sometimes people want a forelock. Of course, I would have my horse mounted and stuffed in my living room."

Exhaustion is a normal state during the busy season.

***

Earlier that evening, a Thoroughbred foal had come in for Dr. Bryan Waldridge after a difficult delivery on the farm. Although at first the newborn filly had stood well and nursed, she had since regressed, unable to do either.

She was a big baby, the largest foal I'd ever seen, with a heavy coat. (Dr. Bonnie Barr once told me that nature's intelligence always impresses her: Foals born in the colder months always have the thickest hair.) The foal didn't get enough oxygen during birth and her gastrointestinal tract wasn't quite mature enough to move the milk through in a normal way. Her body needed a little time to catch up. She was being fed intravenously, and Waldridge was going to try to get her to nurse again. She had also been given plasma (the fluid portion of the blood containing nutrients and proteins) to help boost her immune system.

In the ICU Waldridge had just gotten the foal's bloodwork back from the lab.

"It's all pretty good," he said, handing the results to Dr. Julie Wolfe, an intern. "Her IgGs are better than 16." He was referring to the antibodies a foal receives from its mother in her colostrum, the special milk produced within the twenty-four hours following birth. Waldridge meant 1,600 milligrams per deciliter; above 800 is considered good.

"That's awesome," Wolfe replied.

Across from Waldridge the foal tried to get up off the bed. "There she goes!" the vet said.

But the foal collapsed back on the mattress. "That thing's gigantic," said the vet. The foal splayed its legs and then slid off the bed. Waldridge went into the stall. "C'mon, baby. Gotta get you up." With a heave, he quickly got her to her feet. The foal tottered over to her mom. Because of her height, she had to bend her head down to try to nurse. She latched on and started to feed. Upright, her legs looked almost as sturdy as an adult horse.

"God, you need a forklift for that thing," Waldridge said. "She must weigh 130 pounds." (The average weight of a newborn Thoroughbred foal is 100 to 120 pounds.)

It was Waldridge's third foaling season at Rood & Riddle. The vet has a *Saturday Night Live* sense of humor (favorite movie: *Blues Brothers*) and a relaxed Southern manner that dovetails with a thirsty, scientific mind. He's published papers with colleagues on everything from stomach cancer in llamas to how to determine at-risk pregnancies in mares. He was the first of his family to leave Kentucky when he went to veterinary school at Auburn and spent five years there as a professor before coming to Rood & Riddle in 2005. In the ICU that night I asked Waldridge if he had to prepare himself psychologically for the demands of foaling season. "You just know for five months you can't do anything," he said. "I thought I worked hard before."

The ICU is an enclosed, rectangular room, about 50-by-60 feet, surrounded by stalls. (Two smaller rooms branch off the far end, holding medications, supplies, and the mattresses, pillows, and pads used for the foals, as well as a washer and dryer to launder their bedding.) A long station sits in the middle of the large room; from it, vets and techs update charts, make phone calls, and consult with each other. One of the first nights I sat at the station a tech told me about the time a mare delivered a foal that looked like a mythical creature, with two heads and seven legs (it did not live).

Waldridge finished up with the big filly and checked on another patient diagonally across from her that looked like a foal from another planet. Its forehead was all puffed up, its eyes swollen and too big for its head. Her birth had been a dystocia. One of the foal's legs had been malpositioned, and the fragile skin under her armpit had been lacerated on her way out of the uterus, allowing air into her body's subcutaneous tissue (tissue just beneath the surface of the skin), puffing her up "like a marshmallow," as Wolfe put it. (Waldridge said you could "hear her squish when you picked her up.") A surgeon had sutured the laceration, and with some time and medication the puffiness would likely dissipate. As a result, however, this foal, too, was delayed when it came to knowing how to nurse.

Waldridge finished checking on his other patients and went home. Twenty-five feet away in the adjacent barn, a mare heavy with life paced in her stall. She was on Foal Watch, being checked every fifteen minutes. She had been pregnant now a full year. Eleven months is considered the standard length of time for equine gestation, although that can vary depending on the mare. Still, the mare's owner considered her way overdue and was anxious because of her history: In the past four years she'd had a cesarean, a

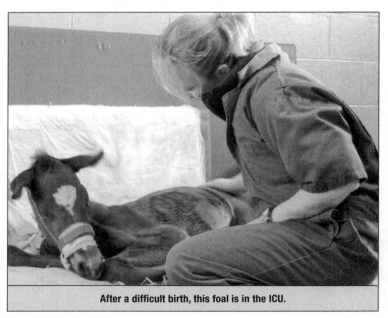

After a difficult birth, this foal is in the ICU.

dystocia, a pregnancy where she hemorrhaged and almost died …
and another year when she was unable to conceive. (When I later
told a friend outside the Bluegrass about this mare, she wanted to
know why the farm would put her through another pregnancy. The
answer is that for this Bluegrass Thoroughbred farm and any farm
that makes its living from breeding horses, broodmare wombs are
"miniature economies.") The mare was Barr's patient, and the vet
was worried about what might happen.

***

At 4 a.m. the Foal Watch mare started to have her baby. To everyone's relief, it was quick and easy, like cracking an egg. Dr. Albert
Solé Guitart delivered the baby, with help from fellow interns Julie
Wolfe and Sarah Gray. Wolfe checked in on Waldridge's big filly
in ICU next door right after the birth, around 5 a.m. She was colicking. It was mild, but Wolfe was a little worried. She muzzled
her so she wouldn't nurse anymore. Keeping anything more out of
her stomach would allow her system to rest and give it the time it
needed to try to start successfully working on its own again.

At 5:30 a.m. I caught up with Dr. Birthe Pegel, another intern, doing rounds. She was checking on a big, dark bay show horse recovering from two surgeries for severe colic. The horse was one of the
big names of his world. He was so temperamental, his groom was
coming to the hospital regularly to spiff him up; the horse wouldn't
let anyone else do it. He had an entourage that visited often. Fans
had found out the horse was in the hospital, and a false rumor
had surfaced he was dead. Sometimes famous horses are admitted
into the clinic under assumed names, like two-footed celebrities in
regular hospitals, although this one had not.

The horse tried to bite Pegel. He didn't like to be touched, and she
was listening to his gut through her stethoscope for any sounds of
potential problems (for example, gas distension, especially in the

colon, makes a *pling* sound like a Jamaican steel drum). Pegel finished up and checked on a few other patients. Then I followed her up to the conference room for the weekly meeting of the interns' Journal Club, where one of the staff veterinarians conducts a seminar on a particular subject. This week, Barr was discussing neonatal equine medicine. As Barr set up her slide show, interns attacked the big bag of assorted bagels she had brought for breakfast.

Barr started out discussing septicemia and went on to discuss numerous other topics related to neonates. Toward the end of her talk she said, "Each foal is its own pharmacological situation … in coming up with a treatment plan, it's important to be assessing very frequently. Things can change. Sometimes, changes can be subtle. If a tech calls you and says, 'This foal's doing this,' don't blow them off. Little things can turn out to be *big* problems."

At the exact time Barr was saying this, the big filly down in ICU took a turn for the worse. Her colic went from mild to severe. She started rolling on her back, a sign of intense pain. She had an ileus, meaning her intestine had stopped moving. Fluid was building up in her bowel, stretching the intestinal walls. Waldridge put her on fluids and various medications intravenously. She'd have to be constantly monitored; she was not only prone to septicemia, she could die from a rupture. A little thing had turned into a big problem.

***

No matter what time of day, the hospital is full of sounds: scrubbing, scrubbing, and more scrubbing … workers clean operating rooms, barns, stalls, entryways, and examining rooms. Hay rustles as horses feed, water drips from hoses and faucets, hooves clip across asphalt as clinicians conduct lameness exams. You hear the crinkly sound of granola bars being unwrapped by famished interns (staff veterinarians never eat, as far as I can tell), the gabbing of a flock of birds that nests in the three evergreen trees by Barn 7.

The P.A. system constantly interrupts conversations, as it did after Saturday morning melted into lunchtime during these twenty-four hours: Embertson was being paged. A 1,400-pound warmblood had arrived from Indiana. He had gotten a leg caught in a gate. The laceration wasn't serious, but it needed to be stitched up. In the admissions office, his owner, bossy in her worry, wanted an MRI. The admissions staff told her regular X-rays would probably suffice, and they did.

In the surgery area, interns readied the horse for Embertson. On the gurney, the warmblood looked even bigger than he did when standing.

"The table needs to be brought up," said Dr. Leslie Christnagel,

Sanitation and disinfection are top priorities at the hospital.

who was running the anesthesia, to Dr. Alexandra Tracey.

Tracey bent down and pressed the button that raised it electronically. The table jerked, rose, and then came off its hydraulic wheels a bit, as occasionally happens, tilting the table slightly and putting the horse on an angle. Everyone jumped.

Embertson walked up.

"It looks like that horse is going off the table. We need to drop him down," Embertson said. (An intern from a previous year told me Embertson often pointed out to interns what they felt they already knew, and they loved to tease him for it. This intern's affectionate nickname for the surgeon is Captain Obvious.)

The interns fixed the table, and Embertson put on his headlamp and sat down on a chair in front of the horse's injured leg. With a scalpel he peeled back the skin of the laceration, and then with surgical scissors he started removing any dead, contaminated, or traumatized tissue. Tracey and Dr. Milosz Grabski assisted him.

The interns were high on sugar. The hospital's weight-loss contest had ended the night before, and they had spent the last fourteen hours or so eating as much chocolate as possible. As they all worked, the giddy intern threesome speed-talked to Embertson about everything from Dr. Alan Ruggles' self-confidence (His favorite phrase: "One time I was wrong, but it was a mistake.") to Christnagel's engineer boyfriend texting her about his breakfast getting ruined in the toaster ("The biojelly Pop Tarts have a thermal expansion issue.").

Embertson finished up and anchored in a drain to draw off excess fluid. Then he pulled the two biggest edges of the skin toward each other over the open wound and the drain. A gap existed in the middle. "It's going to be a little tight," the vet said. Then, slowly and carefully, he sutured the wound, solving the puzzle of how to close the gap with the existing skin step-by-step. He did so by looking for different angles to align and by finding which parts of the skin stretched and which did not. In the end, the wound was almost completely sewn up. Only a tiny gap, less than an eighth of an inch, remained on one corner.

In the recovery stall Christnagel and Grabski waited for the horse to wake up to help him out of the anesthesia while I talked to Tracey as she cleaned up. At Rood & Riddle, to "recover" a horse from anesthesia, one rope is tied to the horse's halter, another to its tail, and both ropes go through metal rings in the wall to act as a pulley system. One person (in this case Grabski) waits at the hind end of the horse holding the rope at the ready, while another (Christnagel) sits on its neck, looking for signs that it is waking: eyes become alert; the horse begins to swallow; the tongue regains its tone. Shortly after these signs appear, the horse usually begins to try to get up. Both people help by pulling on the ropes to stabilize the animal.

It sounds easier than it is. Recovering a horse is a dangerous and unpredictable task. Horses are creatures of flight; their first instinct upon waking up confused in a strange place is to try to get out of there as quickly as possible. A horse often becomes conscious of its surroundings before all of its body wakes up, and it will try to rise, usually front end first. It could hurt itself, but because a horse can't rise without lifting its head, the recoverer on the neck can slow the process by holding down the head. Finally, some horses coming to have a stronger flight response than others and try to rise before the telltale signs of waking appear.

As I talked to Tracey, out of the blue Christnagel yelled, "You GUYS!!!" The warmblood was trying to get up without the vets having gotten good notice. He lifted and turned his head toward the wall as he tried to rise, taking Christnagel with him and encircling her with his neck. He was too strong for her to hold down. The danger existed of him throwing her into the middle of the stall and then stepping on top of her. When he turned his neck away from the wall for a moment, Christnagel darted out and grabbed his halter rope. In the next five minutes or so, with the help of the interns, the horse staggered to his feet and urinated.

The owner came in. "He got up pretty quick," Tracey told her with a straight face. As the owner cooed baby talk to the horse, her husband waited outside the stall with a resigned look. He rolled his eyes at me and said, "It's out of control. One time during a storm, she wanted to bring him into the basement, and I said, 'That is *not* gonna happen.' "

***

Waldridge's extra-large filly fought her colic for twelve hours and won. In the ICU she was weak but stable. The puffy foal across from her was learning how to nurse ("starting to figure out the udder zone," Waldridge said). It was now early Saturday evening.

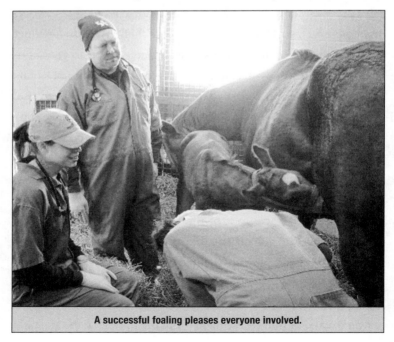

A successful foaling pleases everyone involved.

Waldridge had been working virtually thirty-six hours straight. He went home, and as he was getting ready to grab a shower, the clinic rang: Come back. Dystocia.

An hour is considered the maximum time to get a foal out alive (with rare exceptions) from the time water breaks, and by the time this mare got to Rood & Riddle, it had already been twenty minutes. Tucked inside its mother, the foal's head was pointed down toward its chin and then turned to one shoulder, instead of the normal position of head extended between front legs reaching forward (with back legs pointing straight behind). The hospital staff went into what I thought of as the dystocia ballet. The choreography unfolded: Within three minutes the mare was anesthetized and hoisted in the air upside-down. Three to four more minutes passed during which Dr. Travis Tull reached into the mare's uterus, took hold of the baby's mandible (lower jawbone) with his thumb and forefinger, and positioned the head correctly. Straps were attached to the baby's front feet, which were already protruding from the mother. As two interns pulled on the straps, Tull used his hands to guide and ensure that the head remained extended in the pelvic canal. In a few more seconds, the baby was out.

At a nearby gurney, Waldridge and Wolfe waited in white jumpsuits that made them look like workers in a nuclear power plant. The jumpsuits are made of a biosecure material that helps ensure nothing contaminates newborns. Tull's team quickly handed over the filly and she was placed on the gurney. Wolfe clamped and cut the umbilicus; Waldridge inserted nasotracheal tubes and assisted the foal's breathing with an ambu bag. While techs wiped the filly clean and rubbed her to facilitate breathing, Wolfe and a tech got a catheter in the foal's neck to administer medication if she ran into trouble. But the foal's heartbeat was strong. Soon, she was breathing on her own.

Less than twenty minutes later, Wolfe was helping the new filly learn to walk. A nursemare (equine wet nurse) was being arranged; the foal's mother was considered a risky candidate for nursing because of previous health problems. The foal was so cute she looked like a stuffed animal from FAO Schwartz: small, red, two long, perfectly matched white socks, a blaze down her forehead in the shape of a dagger. It's hard to remember something so adorable is actually an investment that can cost someone $100,000 or more. As the foal tried to walk, she kept getting too close to the wall, almost bumping into it several times. When Wolfe put her hands on her, her skin rippled, having never felt a human's touch.

Waldridge stopped by the stall before he went back home.

"I like little red horses," he mused, looking at the foal.

Wolfe wanted the baby to take a rest, but the foal wanted to keep walking.

"She doesn't listen," Wolfe said.

"She's female," Waldridge replied.

"That's why I like fillies." Wolfe said, "They can push through anything."

The two vets watched the foal, and the other mares in the unit watched their foals. Another foal would arrive during an ice storm in critical respiratory distress at 4 a.m. for Waldridge, followed by a mare two hours later with severe colic for Embertson. The foal would be saved. The mare with colic would fall down on the frozen asphalt after exiting the trailer, unable to rise. Interns would have to put her on a glide and drag her in to surgery, slipping and sliding all over the place. After surgery, that horse would also live. The rest of the weekend would bring more emergencies, more lost sleep. But right now inside the ICU unit, it was calm, and outside, the sky contemplated darkness.

CHAPTER

2

Enigmas

It is an early April morning, and I am driving with Dr. Kathleen Paasch and a tech out to Claiborne Farm near Paris, Kentucky. She's been using acupuncture to treat a yearling with undescended testicles, and I'm going to watch her do a treatment. Acupuncture is something a proud left-brainer like Paasch had difficulty embracing at first. In addition to college, vet school, and a year interning at Rood & Riddle before being hired, Paasch had also managed along the way to pick up a PhD in sociology. In another life, she worked as a federal statistician. She is the daughter of a nurse and an Air Force navigator. Acupuncture does not fit with the template of who she is. But when she became a vet, clients wanted it for their horses, so she got certified, although she focuses on orthopedics and lameness.

Paasch discovered that acupuncture works, and it bugs her because she doesn't understand how. She prefers studying conformation (a horse's build) and reading X-rays to working with energy meridians, tongue pulses, and *chi*, the life force central to acupuncture. Paasch is easy to banter with. When I asked her how the yearling was responding to the treatment, she replied, "It looks like it's working," somewhat glumly. Then when I dubbed her The Reluctant Acupuncturist, she laughed and said, "It works," as she whipped her gray SUV onto Paris Pike in the rain. "So I do it."

One of the fundamental principles of acupuncture is that releasing blocked energy (*chi*) across various channels in the body (meridians) results in healing, bringing the body into balance. In China it has been used on horses for more than 3,000 years. It is easy to forget as modern people that tending to equine health was once a necessity around the globe. For centuries, horses were public transportation, farm equipment, expeditionary vehicles, and the seat upon which wars were fought. For instance, when Catherine the Great traveled 1,000 miles in 1787 from St. Petersburg, Russia, to the Crimea with the unsuccessful plan of conquering the Ottoman Empire, she and her huge entourage did not travel in a convoy of tanks. They spent hours taking care of their transportation each time they stopped for the night.

In China, one of the fathers of equine acupuncture was a brainy, hard-working equine veterinarian named Sun Yang (nickname: Bole) who lived from 659 to 621 B.C. His skill at adapting acupuncture to horses and treating multiple equine diseases resulted in the first book of its kind: *Bole's Canon of Veterinary Acupuncture*. During Sun's time, because of the importance of horses for war and everyday life, the job of an equine vet was a respected career, apparently one of the highest in society. In the land of the Bluegrass, equine vets are also highly regarded. Kentucky-bred horses make up roughly a quarter of all the Thoroughbreds that race in the United States and Canada, earning millions of dollars. Vets here such as Paasch swoop in, fixing valuable horses in a single bound. Paasch is in her mid-forties; she has hay-blonde hair and is willowy and athletic, a snow-skiing, snorkeling, fly-fishing vet. All of that was much easier to do out West, where she went to vet school, than it is now for her in Kentucky, where she

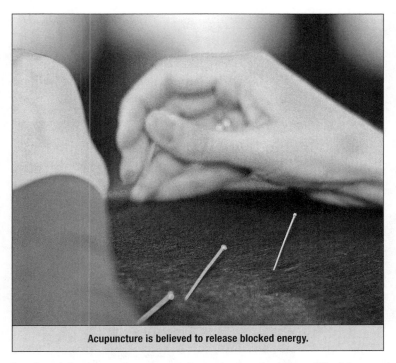

Acupuncture is believed to release blocked energy.

has lived for about ten years since graduating from Washington State University's program in 1999.

After graduation, Paasch found an enormous amount of skepticism among fellow vets when it came to acupuncture. In a decade all that has changed, with almost every major vet school including it in the curriculum. Equine vets use acupuncture to treat everything from laminitis to fertility problems in mares and stallions. Paasch received her certification from the International Veterinary Acupuncture Society, started by three vets in 1974. At acupuncture school in San Diego, Paasch and the sixty or so other similarly wary vets were told right off, "We're not telling you to abandon your Western practice; this is to complement it." Everyone seemed relieved, Paasch said. Still, I wonder what they thought of some of the curriculum:

The roots of Chinese medicine are in the science of Taoism, and the

Taoist classics hold profound insights of use in Chinese medicine. The Tao De Jing states that:

"The Tao gives birth to the One: The One gives birth to the Two; The Two gives birth to the Three; The Three gives birth to the Ten Thousand Things."

In this passage, the One is the undifferentiated Essence, full of potential. This Essence, or Tao, differentiates into the two fundamental forces, Yin and Yang. When Yin and Yang interact, they produce a life force. This life force then animates everything on earth, the Ten Thousand Things. This interaction is the foundation of life ...

Claiborne Farm is steeped in history and tradition.

When I first read that, I had a hard time imagining being an equine vet in Kentucky and talking with owners, trainers, and farm managers about how the Ten Thousand Things would help them win a graded stakes race. But Paasch told me that horse people can be as mysti- cal as Kabbalists and as super- stitious as baseball players. I learned this later on in the year when I met many people who would only wean and geld (cas- trate) their horses under certain cycles of the moon, thought to be more harmonious for a suc- cessful outcome.

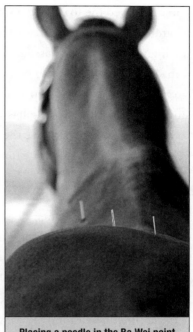

Placing a needle in the Ba Wei point (center) has numerous benefits.

Claiborne, where Paasch and I were headed, is one of the old- est and most historic farms in the Bluegrass, run by the Hancock family since 1915. If beauty is God's handwriting, as Ralph Waldo Emerson put it, then Claiborne is a letter from above. Three thou- sand acres dotted with yellow and white barns; mares, foals, and stallions grazing in paddocks with grass so perfect it looks as if it is combed every morning. Seabiscuit was foaled here. Big Brown's sire, Boundary, was conceived here, as was Secretariat; both retired from racing to stand at stud at Claiborne. One of the farm's late leading sires, Princequillo, was brought to the United States from Europe during World War II, his ship dodging Ger- man submarines. We pulled into the farm and drove up to one of the barns, where yearling manager Charlie Rimer met us with a horse he asked me to call Get Over It. The colt was a cryptorchid, meaning one or both testicles had stayed up in the abdomen or the inguinal canal, the passage route into the abdomen and scrotum. In Get Over It's case, both testicles were undescended. No surgical treatment exists to make them descend. However, in a situation where one testicle has dropped, and the other has not, some owners will opt to have the latter removed surgically if they believe the condition affects a racehorse's performance by causing discomfort.

In Get Over It's case, Paasch was using acupuncture coupled with hormone treatments; she got the two-pronged approach from Rood & Riddle veterinarian Dr. Debbie Spike-Pierce, who says the combination is more effective than either one alone. If the approach didn't work, which can happen, and the colt remained a "crypt," he would be considered damaged goods when it came time to sell him, although that is often more perception than reality. In 2004, Rimer told me, Claiborne sold a double crypt yearling (both testicles undescended) for a client at the Keeneland September sale for $32,000. Four years later the horse had won $300,000 and counting. "A true horseman won't be scared off" by a cryptorchid, says Rimer. Some famous stallions in Bluegrass breeding sheds are single crypts, although their owners don't publicize it because some people will always believe that when it comes to testicles, a matched set is best.

Get Over It was the first cryptorchid at Claiborne ever treated with acupuncture. The year before, the farm had sold a crypt yearling it had raised for $20,000. The buyer had one of the testicles removed surgically, put the colt in a sale for two-year-olds in training, and sold him for $700,000. Rimer said it was a lesson learned, but he always sees surgery — any surgery — as a last resort. No matter how advanced equine anesthetic techniques have become, and how skillful

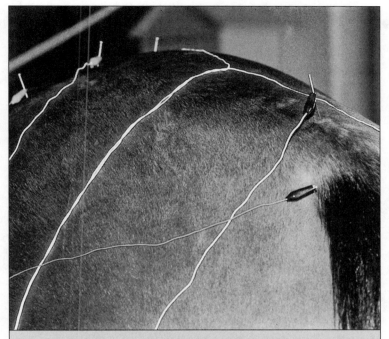

Mild electrical stimulation of the points can make the treatment more effective.

the surgeon is doing a procedure, putting a horse under and cutting him open always carries danger. As Rimer says, "If you do the acupuncture without results you're not out much, and you're damned sure not out the horse."

Get Over It was jumpy. Paasch tranquilized him so he'd stand for the treatment and to reduce the likelihood of her getting kicked. She started by placing a needle in the Ba Wei point on the top of the colt's rump. It's a governing-body point, meaning it is designed to raise the level of overall health. It also releases endorphins, producing a feeling of calmness, and helps with reproductive issues, as did all the subsequent points she put in: two inside the hock, two on the back, and one above the right front hoof. In the acupuncture education Paasch received, traditional points developed by the Chinese specifically for animals are used, as are "transpositional points," those based on corresponding points in humans. Western veterinary research into neurophysiology and neuroanatomy contribute to new points all the time. Paasch used fine-gauge hypodermic needles and injected the hormone, called GnRH, into the needle right after it was inserted in the point; GnRH (gonadotropin-releasing hormone) is thought to help release natural testosterone, which may in turn lead to the testes dropping.

After a short while, Paasch put electrodes on some of the points and plugged the slender cords attached to them into a small device that gives a mild electrical stimulation — doing so is believed to make the treatment stronger. Another way of stimulating a point is through moxibustion, where an herb called moxa is burned on top of the needle, heating it up and stimulating the point. But Paasch said, "I'm not very good with fire ... plus there's hair, fur, hay ... that smell of incense. I just don't go there."

Acupuncture is an art, and practitioners find their own creative ways of developing treatments within its framework. For example, at a couple of other farms, managers asked Paasch if she thought acupuncture would help with horses that weave — which is when a stalled horse shifts its weight and moves its head back and forth out of boredom, anxiety, or both (in Spain, horse people call it "the sway of the bear"). She thought about it and decided to put a single staple in a point on each of the horse's foreheads. The intent is to induce calming, and the staples stay in until they fall out, between three and eight weeks. Although it sounds like it would hurt, it doesn't, and is similar to more sustained treatments for humans. Out of approximately twelve horses, seven stopped weaving.

Back at Claiborne, Paasch took the needles out of the colt and checked his testicles. Since the last treatment, the right one had al-

The 1973 Triple Crown winner is buried in a place of honor.

ready started to drop and was continuing to do so — in size and shape, the testicle felt normal, about the size of a goose egg — and it seemed to Paasch as if the left one might be dropping now as well.

***

With the acupuncture done, Rimer asked us if we wanted to see The Shed. By this he meant the breeding shed where six out of the eleven Triple Crown winners were conceived. Claiborne is superstitious about The Shed. Other farms have more glamorous-looking breeding sheds with features such as viewing platforms for small audiences. But Claiborne doesn't want to fool with the mysticism and success of The Shed. Like all the farm's barns, it is simple: literally just a great big shed — black rubber scraps on the floor (to give the stallion traction and cushioning), some windows, padded walls. (A Claiborne farm manager once said, when showing a *Lexington Herald-Leader* reporter around, "I can't show you the million-dollar barn, but I can show you the million-dollar horse.") On the way there, Paasch told me it was only recently that Claiborne permitted women to enter The Shed because it clashes with the farm's sense of propriety, and some women connected with the farm still stay away out of respect for that tradition.

When we arrived, four or five men were getting ready to help an aroused stallion mount (or cover, as it's called) a mare. The mare wasn't cooperating; handlers held her still with a twitch, a pole with a loop at the end that twists around the fleshy part of the nose, restraining the horse. After a few extremely unromantic heaving moments, with the crew urging the stallion on like the entourage for a heavyweight champ in the ring, the deed was done.

Next, Rimer wanted to show us two horse cemeteries. On a grassy plot not far from the shed is the farm's main burial ground. The tradition for burying a racehorse is to bury just the head, the heart, and the hooves, considered the soul of the animal. But at Claiborne some are buried whole, such as Triple Crown legend Secretariat. Also buried whole was Swale, who died of a heart attack during a bath ten days after winning the 1984 Belmont Stakes. He was put to rest with his garland of Derby-winning roses around his neck.

A short drive away is Marchmont, another cemetery, with granite headstones for stallions such as Ack Ack, Unbridled, Easy Goer, and Drone, and for the broodmares Moccasin, Thong, and Tuerta, the one-eyed filly and stakes-winning mother of Swale. Next to a marker for champion Banshee Breeze, who died having her first foal, is Pine Island's grave. She lived from 2003 to 2006, and was conceived and foaled at the farm. She was owned by the Phipps family, the American racing dynasty now in its fourth generation. The family boards all its broodmares and foals at Claiborne. "She was homely," said Rimer of Pine Island. "She had terrible conformation. People said, 'You have got to sell this horse.' But that horse had a lot of heart." Heart is a word horse people don't throw around; it denotes a specific kind of horse, one with a luminous will to compete and win.

Rimer recounted that when a Rood & Riddle veterinarian would come out periodically to look at Pine Island's conformation when she was young, the vet would say, "They're not all meant to be athletes, Charlie."

But she was. According to Rimer, "She was the kind you want to root for. She went out there and tried so hard every time she put her foot on the racetrack. She was just happy-go-lucky, nothing bothered her. Most horses when thrown off guard and off balance, they react, usually not in a good way. They're creatures of flight that want to get out of situations by themselves. Very few horses will trust people to take care of them. She did."

Pine Island raced only a year and won more than $600,000. In the backstretch of the 2006 Breeders' Cup Distaff at Churchill Downs, she took a misstep and dislocated her left front fetlock joint. The bone broke the skin and she had to be euthanized after the race. (Pine Island's jockey, Javier Castellano, flipped over her head but was unhurt.) Grief covered the farm like the 1,000 sycamores planted by Arthur Hancock Sr. (at twenty-five cents a piece) in the farm's beginnings in the early 1900s.

It is too early to tell if Get Over It has heart, but by summer, he was no longer a cryptorchid. Claiborne kept the colt and put him in training, with hopes to race him at the 2009 Keeneland fall meet. He was the tenth cryptorchid Paasch has successfully treated, making her more of a believer in acupuncture. Still, she doesn't know precisely how it works anymore than Rimer knows how to predict if a foal will have what it takes on the inside to be a member of Claiborne's equinocracy.

"You'll hope it's there," Rimer said, "but you really can't tell when they're being raised on the farm. It's only until they get engaged in a head-to-head battle, you see how they come through that. You never know, the John Henrys, the horses like that. You never know. It is a mystery. That's what keeps everybody going in this business from top to bottom, they don't have to be the biggest or the richest, but they can still come up with that one special horse.

"You can have a perfect specimen of a horse and all the modern technology in the world, but you still cannot see or measure a horse's heart."

Thrilling

The Standardbred mare hung upside-down, anesthetized, suspended by an electric hoist. Dr. Pedro de Pedro and Dr. Scott Hopper were struggling to pull out her foal with canvas straps they'd tied to the baby's two front ankles, which protruded from the mare's vagina. It had been about twenty minutes since the mare's water had broken, and with each minute that passed the chances of the foal being born alive decreased. The vets thought they might have to rush to a C-section. Outside the stall, Dr. Steve Reed and a medical team stood next to a gurney, ready to grab the baby and treat it for cardiac or respiratory distress if the other vets could pull it out. The mare's name was Victor's Pursuit, and it was her first foal.

The baby was big, and Victor's Pursuit small, a light bay with a star on her forehead and a stripe down the middle of her face. The correct orientation for a foal to come into the world is as a diver, head between both front extended legs and feet. This foal was twisted in the uterus, lying on its side. Its chest was deep. All this made the journey to leave the uterus difficult. No natural lubrication remained to help ease its passage — too much time had lapsed from the point at which the mare's water had broken and now. Because the birth canal and uterus had been so sticky and rough, Hopper had pumped in a couple liters of lubricant. He had reached in and pushed the foal out of the birth canal back into the uterus (a procedure called repulsion), and then manipulated it into the correct position. Now, as he and de Pedro pulled on the obstetrical straps, he hoped the foal was still alive.

Hopper, a surgeon at Rood & Riddle since 1998, had attended to countless dystocias (difficult births) before this one, but for de Pedro, an intern, emergencies were still new … and one of the reasons he had recently switched from equine podiatry to internal medicine.

De Pedro is around thirty years old and from Puerto Rico. His grandfather put him on his first horse at three years old, he was riding alone at four, and bought his first mare (pregnant) at twelve (he still has the foal: Topaz). He had been a farrier before veterinary school, and had been certain he would go straight into podiatry afterward in a private practice. But one of his best friends, Dr. Raul Bras, works at Rood & Riddle and convinced him to apply for an internship after graduation. He was accepted, did one internship out in the field, and was now doing a second in internal medicine. Equine podiatry can be complex, and de Pedro loved the challenge of correcting other farriers' work and handling horses. But he quickly found that working in medicine is more of a rush: In emergencies, it is like when "they turn on the lights in the baseball park," he says. "People come alive. You've got to get going no matter how many hours you've slept." Yet he also loves the calm that is required, the evenness of the staff in the jaggedness of the moment. After his internship, he would go on to do a residency in equine medicine and surgery at the University of Illinois at Urbana-Champaign.

Back with the mare, Hopper and de Pedro got out one of the foal's front legs and its body midway to the thorax. De Pedro lifted its lip to check the mucous membranes of the gums. In a healthy foal with

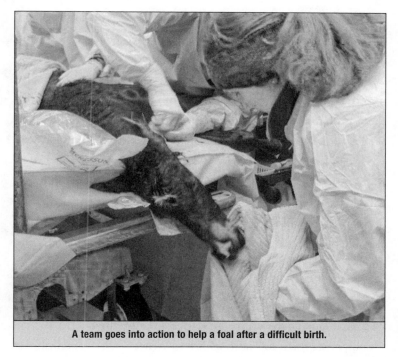

A team goes into action to help a foal after a difficult birth.

good, oxygenated blood flow, the membranes are pink. This foal's membranes were purple and black.

***

The mare, Victor's Pursuit, was six years old. A year earlier, a suspensory injury in Florida put an end to her harness racing career. She had earned over a quarter million dollars. Her most recent owner, Bill Weaver, lives on the East Coast but boards the mare near Georgetown, Kentucky, at Peninsula Farm. By his own admission, Weaver spoils his horses; one, for example, likes only Green Giant carrots, which he willingly provides. He calls Victor's Pursuit a Tiffany mare and a sweetheart.

Weaver got into harness racing in its heyday forty-five years ago. He was working on Wall Street at the time. In New York, he hung out at Yonkers and Roosevelt raceways (the latter closed in 1988).

But when he had to make a bet equal to a week's pay to break even, he said, "This is *not* for me." He went into the military service, and when he got out the Standardbred world continued to beckon, so he wrote letters to people in the business, trying to find an entrée. He received only one letter back, but fortunately it was from Stanley Dancer, the most successful harness racer and trainer of his time. Dancer, a driven eighth-grade dropout who survived multiple serious racing accidents, won over $28 million in his career (he died in 2005). After he and Weaver got together, Dancer put him in touch with his trainer nephew, to whom Weaver quickly entrusted two horses. One of those horses ended up coming in second in the 1969 Hambletonian, a.k.a. the Hambo, the Kentucky Derby of harness racing. It was the beginning of a long career that hasn't always been as easy as its start. Weaver also worked as a banker and did well enough to go out on his own with Standardbreds, breeding and training, as long as he kept an eye on costs. Now, he's semi-retired.

Comparing them to Thoroughbreds, Weaver calls Standardbreds "more durable ... coarser, heartier, probably more kid-friendly. More even-tempered." In the earliest days of harness racing, around the late 1800s, some Standardbreds at the track were in their second careers; the first was pulling milk wagons.

The sire of Victor's Pursuit went unraced, but her grand-sire, Valley Victory, was a superstar. He's retired now in Kentucky. In the 1980s and '90s, Valley Victory earned almost half a million dollars and sired countless trotters that won millions, and they sired more that won even more millions. In 1989, he was unbeaten and expected to win the Hambletonian against rival Peace Corps, a filly. Both were sired by the same father. One week before the race, Valley Victory caught a viral infection running through his barn. His owner, a former court reporter, made the decision not to run him three days before the race and a half-hour before the final deadline to enter. The harness racing world was in shock, as if Muhammad Ali had cancelled on George Foreman for the Rumble in the Jungle. Valley Victory went to stud afterward.

During his race career, Valley Victory knew he was hot stuff. In recalling his temperament in 2007 in an online article, his trainer, Steve Elliott, said, "That horse was so full of himself." When he gave the interview, Elliott had just won the Hambletonian for the first time, with a horse named Donato Hanover, eighteen years after trying to do so with Valley Victory. Valley Victory had been a "precocious kid," he said, while Donato Hanover was more of a professional.

Valley Victory was redeemed from his Hambletonian disappointment, in a way, when two sons, a daughter, and a grandson won the Hambletonian themselves. One breeding manager told an online racing publication that Valley Victory's descendants are noted for calm attitudes, flexibility, and just plain niceness. "Whatever you ask doesn't seem to be problem for them," he said. When Valley Victory's granddaughter and the foal inside her arrived at Rood & Riddle, the two were asked to give it everything they had.

***

Teresa Duer is the farm manager at Peninsula Farm, where Victor's Pursuit boards. The farm was started by her father, Carter Duer, and she's been working there more than twenty-five years. Sometimes she gets uneasy feelings about certain mares when they are about to give birth. As Victor's Pursuit got close to foaling, she lay quietly in her stall, which is normal. But Duer felt inexplicably worried. Then Stan Tokarchick, the farm's maintenance man, was driving by the paddock and saw the mare out in the field, starting to foal. It was during the day; 80 percent of mares foal at night. He went out and saw the amnion, the white placental membrane encasing the foal, protruding from the vulva, marking the end of the first stage of labor. In about five minutes, her water would break when the amnion ruptured. He immediately got the mare into the barn. The first thing Duer always does is check for the position of a foal's feet. First off, the feet were upside-down, and then she couldn't get her fingers around them, they were so big. "Oh my gosh," she said. "Stan, you get the truck and trailer."

Duer's farm is five minutes from Rood & Riddle. The mare and foal medical teams were waiting at the clinic when they arrived. Within minutes, Victor's Pursuit was anesthetized in a padded stall and hoisted into the air. As Duer watched Hopper and de Pedro work on her, time flattened and stretched out. The longer things took, the more scared she got. Then she saw de Pedro pull the foal out. To her, it looked "totally blue."

During the first stage of labor in a normal birth, the foal turns from its back to its belly in the uterus. That can take anywhere from minutes to hours. In the second stage, the water breaks and the foal is birthed, all in about twenty minutes. If more than an hour passes in this stage, oxygen deprivation usually occurs when the umbilical cord breaks or gets kinked when the foal's belly button presses against the mare's pelvis; the foal is then in danger of dying. If the placenta separates before the foal is out, then the foal is deprived of oxygen, also endangering its life. The third stage of labor is the passage of the placenta, usually in three hours or less.

Although a number of conditions can cause dystocias, the most common is an abnormally positioned foal that cannot exit the birth canal. The mare's uterus becomes spent from contractions that go nowhere, and then it stops contracting. The list of possible wrong positions, or malpresentations as they're called, is long: One front leg can be bent back … the head can be turned to the side … the baby can be positioned rump first. In Milton Toby's biography of the late Colonel Floyd Sager, who was one of the world's most well-known equine vets and the chief vet at Claiborne Farm for almost forty years, Sager said one of the worst abnormal positions he would run into was when a foal had one or both hind feet up against its chest.

"That sort of thing doesn't happen very often, but when it does, you have to just exert a lot of traction and pull the foal free. A few times, I've even had to use a tractor to pull a foal," Sager said, referring to the obstetrical straps being tied to the very slowly moving tractor. Rood & Riddle vets cringed when I told them this quote because of the likely damage to the mare, and they emphasized that birth by tractor is not a good idea. Sager warned of this, too, but said it was called for as a last resort.

When Toby's 1980 book was written, equine C-sections were not as common as they are now. The factors that have changed since then to make them so successful are the refinement of anesthesia use in horses, the speed and skill with which surgeons do the procedure, and the fact that farm managers and owners get mares to the hospital in time to perform it. (Rood & Riddle's Bluegrass location makes it a broodmare hub, ideal for study and analysis when it comes to dystocias and cesareans. Scholarly papers by the hospital's current and past vets are among the pivotal research in this arena in the past twenty years.)

But when it comes to a vaginal birth, a malpositioned foal has to be manipulated to come through the canal like a diver. If the foal dies inside its mother, vets do either a cesarean to get it out or a fetotomy, where the foal is removed in parts, usually with one or two incisions. With a fetotomy, the danger exists of lacerating the cervix, birth canal, and uterus.

The foal de Pedro held in his arms, halfway out of its mother, was a colt. He had no heartbeat. Part of the left side of his chest was collapsed from what looked like several broken ribs. De Pedro and Hopper pulled the foal completely out and handed it to Reed to put on the gurney. Hopper gave Reed a grim look that said the baby was dead. In a moment, the foal would be put in a green plastic garbage bag and taken to the Livestock Diagnostic Center around the bend from Rood & Riddle to be disposed of or cremated.

The room was still. Then, as Reed looked at the foal on the gurney, he saw something through the concavity caused by the broken ribs. "Oh my God," he thought. "It's still got a heartbeat!" He grabbed a nasotracheal tube and stuck it up the foal's nostril, attached a plastic ambu bag used for resuscitation to the tube, and pumped the bag with his hands.

The baby took a huge breath on his own. Life started and kept on going, as Reed put it. Later, when talking about it, Reed said to me: "How could it not be thrilling?"

***

In the Sager biography, the vet tells of arriving at a barn once to find a foal that was born with an open umbilicus, "and his guts started to pop out just as soon as he hit the ground." Sager's foaling man, Buck Fryman, "had pushed the foal's guts back inside his body, and he was holding the umbilicus closed with his hand." With his other hand, Fryman tried to hold the foal upside-down by its hind legs so Sager could close the wound, but the foal was too heavy. The men used halter shanks to create a makeshift hoist and, keeping the guts in place, hung the foal upside-down while Sager sutured the opening. "And he went on to win a race," Sager said. Valley Victory's foal had a birth that was complicated in a different way, but it was no less dramatic.

A few minutes after the foal began to breathe, he was rushed down to ICU. Reed could see his chest collapsing with every breath. "Boy, this is scary," Reed thought. The broken ribs could puncture the blood vessels inside the chest; they could even puncture the heart. Reed thought about the year before when a foal down in ICU with some broken ribs was doing great, but on day four, one of its ribs stuck a hole in a heart ventricle and it bled to death. Over the next forty-eight hours, Reed talked to Teresa Duer on the phone two or three times day. He always said the same thing: "We could lose this baby at any time."

The foal's lungs were inflated, and over the next few days he was hydrated, kept warm, given supplemental nutrition, and other medical care. He learned how to walk and nurse, gaining strength and co-ordination. His ribs began to mend. Three days after he went down to the ICU, just as he had turned the corner, de Pedro noticed Victor's Pursuit shifting her weight from one front foot to another.

"Cows and women are tough. Mares are delicate," wrote Dr. Phyllis M. Lose, the country's first female equine veterinarian, in her classic book *Blessed Are the Broodmares*. "Such a statement does not always endear me to my female clients, but nothing can alter the truth of the facts ... For all her size, the mare's reproductive system is more fragile and less durable than that of any other mammal of which I know."

Victor's Pursuit started lying down more than usual; she was unwilling to walk. Duer came to the hospital for a visit and the foal was nursing from his mother while she was lying down. Duer was worried and told de Pedro, who was as well. The clinical signs looked like laminitis. De Pedro called Dr. Raul Bras in Rood & Riddle's podiatry department.

"Can you take some radiographs and send them to me?" Bras asked. The X-rays showed the laminae between the hoof and the coffin bone (known as the H-L zone) in the two front feet was approximately 22 millimeters thick; it should have been around 16 to 18 millimeters. The distance between the coffin bone and the hoof wall was increasing, indicating separation. Bras believed the mare had developed laminitis.

Laminitis is one of the deep mysteries of equine medicine, a frightening, bewildering, and sometimes deadly condition affecting the interior structures of a horse's foot. It occurs when the laminae — the

Velcro-like interlocking tissue that holds the hoof wall to the coffin bone and keeps that bottommost bone of the leg in place — become inflamed. As strong as the tissue is, it's also incredibly sensitive to disease states.

When tissue is damaged elsewhere in the horse's body, chemicals — and nobody has yet identified what those chemicals are — release and cause the laminae to break down. Once those bonds weaken, the entire weight of a horse bears down on the hoof capsule(s), and the bones displace. Laminitis is extremely painful. ("Imagine being a ballerina and having your toenails ripped out and then having to stand on them," as one vet tried to describe it to me.) The coffin bone can then sink or rotate, or do both. Laminitis has bedeviled horses and their owners for centuries; in the worst cases, the coffin bone can actually come through the sole of a foot. (Laminitis usually affects the front feet more than the hind because 60 percent of the animal's weight is carried in the front.)

Dr. Scott Morrison of the hospital's podiatry department says many people used to think laminitis was caused by decreased blood flow, but current research seems to be disproving that theory and is focusing on the anatomy and physiology of the laminae, what it needs to stay healthy, and, of course, the precise chemicals that are released that break it down. Morrison said it is possible that the future might hold a laminitis antidote, but nobody can predict when. It won't come fast enough for veterinarians and horse owners.

Many things can trigger laminitis. A difficult birth often sets a mother up for big problems afterward: everything from a ruptured birth canal to a retained placenta, which can quickly cause a bacterial infection. Victor's Pursuit didn't have a retained placenta, but vets believed she did have a uterine infection. That plus post-partum stress were the two factors that likely set her up for laminitis, according to de Pedro.

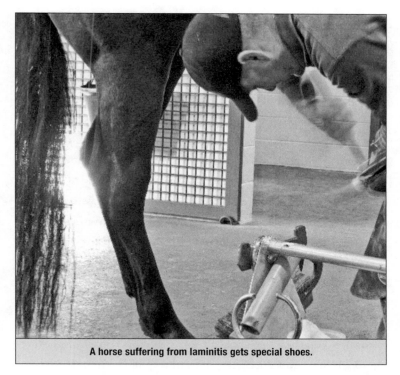

A horse suffering from laminitis gets special shoes.

Along with administering various medications, Bras immediately put the mare in what are called Ultimate Wedge Shoes, designed to release the tension of the tendon pulling on the coffin bone, preventing further damage and rotation. After about a week, she and the foal left the hospital for the farm, with Bras making regular check-ups. For the first twelve weeks at home, Victor's Pursuit was put on stall rest, the equine equivalent of bed rest. She got lower wedges, then special boots, and then another set of therapeutic shoes, all designed for support and protection. Her path from illness to health was uncommon because it followed a straight line. After two months she was well. The foal had limited exercise at first because of his ribs, but also eventually healed completely, developing a friendly, curious personality. Months later, when Bras saw the foal and mare (now pregnant again) healthy and running around Duer's 360-acre farm, he described the scene as "cool as hell."

"They're a great team," he said. "They're just normal horses now."

Unlike many other horses, Victor's Pursuit circumvented a crisis because she was within the hospital ecosystem, being closely watched in ICU with a podiatry department next door. Within twenty-four hours of de Pedro calling Bras, laminitis treatment had started. Time is as critical with laminitis as it would be for a hospital patient with a blood clot. Bras says, for example, "If it was another kind of situation (with a horse on a farm), one vet would ask another vet … that vet would ask another vet … there'd be the trailer ride over here," creating a time lag plus the stress on the mare from the transport.

Sometimes, throughout my year at Rood & Riddle, it was hard not to make the contrast between the health care horses get in Kentucky and the health care people get in our country. The month after Victor's Pursuit's stay at Rood & Riddle, 750 people without health insurance came to a free clinic a couple of hours drive from Lexington to get their eyes checked, rotten teeth pulled, and other basics. Hundreds of people had to be turned away because there weren't enough doctors, time, and supplies to go around. At Rood & Riddle, I never saw anyone wait for hours in the emergency room like you do in a human ER. (The hospital does not turn away an animal in a life-or-death situation either, even if it means the practice has to eat the bill.) Duer said the same thing so many others in the horse world I interviewed said about the equine hospital: "When I get sick, I wish I could come here."

Repro Cowboys

I am trying to find Dr. Chris Newton's house in the morning dark. It is late April, 5:45 a.m., and I am looking for the turnoff that leads to the big tree on the right that I am told marks the driveway to his farm. Newton is one of the ambulatory, or field, veterinarians. When I made plans with him over the phone to come along on farm calls, I asked if he could just pick me up at the hospital because he doesn't live too far away. "No," was the reply, a complete sentence, not rude, just matter-of-fact. I soon learn it is because every second counts. I eventually find the driveway, then find Newton's tech, J.P. Malherbe, in the garage putting the final touches on loading the truck, packed as tight as a space capsule. I jump in hurriedly as instructed, strap in, and a few moments later, at precisely 6:15 a.m., Newton hurtles into the garage and the driver's seat and we lift off, spinning out into the Chris Newton orbit.

All the veterinarians work hard, but Newton one of the hardest: seven days a week, up to eighteen hours a day, thousands of miles a year, call to call to call. (In his free time, between spending it with his wife and two kids, he is a champion equestrian. I wonder: Does he bend time to his will?) As we leave, Malherbe tells me how he is a little tired because the Rolex Kentucky Three-Day Event was the day before, and he and Newton were on the scene assisting when a rider, Laine Ashker, and her horse, Frodo Baggins, went down after failing to clear a fence. (Ashker eventually recovered from serious injuries; Frodo's were so severe he had to be euthanized at Hagyard Equine Medical Institute.) Of course Newton and Malherbe were there, because they are always where the plot is most compelling … together in this battered silver vetcraft, the stainless steel cabinet rattling in the back, a vanilla-colored Buddha sitting in the space between the two front seats, as if its serenity is all that is keeping this thing from splitting like an atom.

Newton is about 5 foot 11, and thinks he looks like (a young) Gene Wilder but not as skinny, and that's about right. He has a trickster quality about him; it's hard to know when he's putting you on, like the time he told me a team of standard poodles once ran the Iditarod (true), or the time he told me one of his horse patients liked chewing tobacco (not true). Like a small-town horse doctor, he relishes getting to know his clients and their crews. He knows every single groom by name and converses with them in Spanish that makes up for stripped-down syntax with its enthusiasm and genuine interest. His stamina comes from his love for the work and the adrenalin he receives from the velocity at which he does it.

Malherbe is an ocean-loving South African from Mossel Bay, a coastal tourist town that draws scuba divers who want to stare down great white sharks from the safety of cages. Malherbe is in his mid-twenties; fit, blond, fast-talking, a citizen of the world conversant in matters of wine and cricket. He used to work for a Saddlebred training barn in Indiana whose clients would fly in on the weekends from all over the country to ride — families with "a seven-year-old on a million-dollar horse with two-karat diamonds in her ears."

In the Chicago airport coming to America several years ago

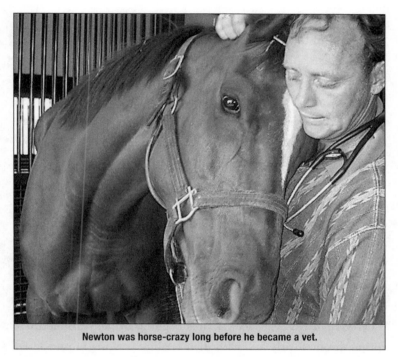

Newton was horse-crazy long before he became a vet.

he got stopped by a modeling agent ready to sign him to catalog work with Abercrombie & Fitch. But he likes Rood & Riddle, even though he could make more money back in Indiana or being photographed in winterwear. He tried being a surgery tech, but there wasn't enough action, and he didn't get to see a case from beginning to end, or talk with clients. He doesn't want to be a tech assigned to internal medicine either, a job spent primarily inside the clinic. He likes the open road with Newton, the vials of drawn blood rattling in his front breast pocket.

Newton specializes in reproduction, but does a multitude of other things: lameness treatment, physical therapy, acupuncture, chiropractic, and special projects such as consulting on the design of a prosthetic hoof. Despite all the aforementioned space metaphors, when it comes down to it, I think of Newton and Malherbe not as

Rood & Riddle's astronauts but as the hospital's cowboys. Riding with them in their truck down country roads, windows open, the breeze tousling the trees, there is a sense of limitlessness and possibility, and the feeling that they can handle whatever comes.

The April trip I take with them, the first of two, is a whirl of mare bottoms. Newton palpates one after the other, reaching up through their rectums to feel around the ovaries. He's looking to see how close to ovulation they are in order to best choose a breeding date. Newton feels for the follicles, small sacs that swell and soften to the size of kiwis about twelve hours before ovulation, when the eggs that wait patiently inside are released. That's the best window during which to breed. Twelve hours after ovulation is too late for a shot at a foal. Newton is also looking for other signs of impending ovulation: The cervix softens, and mucus appears in the vaginal cavity and uterus, which swells as well.

On Mother Nature's clock, mares begin to ovulate around mid-spring through early fall, with their fertility peaking in mid-June. But most everybody in the Thoroughbred world wants a mare pregnant by Derby Day. Pregnancies run roughly eleven months, and earlier foals have more time to grow bigger, stronger, and presumably faster than their later counterparts since racing standards technically deem all their birthdays on January 1. Since 1954, however, only one Kentucky Derby winner has been a January baby, the 1996 champion, Grindstone. But fourteen have been February foals, and fifteen were born in March (these statistics exclude six years where data isn't available). In the quest for a snowtime baby, owners and breeders attempt, as Newton says, "a tug of war with Mother Nature." They try to fool a mare's biological clock. At the beginning of December, lights are kept on in the stalls at night, and the mares are turned out for as long as possible during the day. Doing so makes their reproductive cycles believe the days are getting longer, and if everything goes according to plan, they start ovulating in mid-February. One of my friends lives near a big breeding operation right outside Lexington, and he told me that in winter, with the leaves off the trees, the beams from the barns are so bright that even from a distance they look like searchlights.

One of Rood & Riddle's surgery nurses who gave birth to a baby in 2008 wanted to get pregnant right away again so her kids would be close in age. Staffers kidded her about wanting to be what's called "bred back" in the Thoroughbred world — when breeders attempt to get mares pregnant during foal heat — the two-week period after having a baby when a mare's first estrus or heat begins. This constant cycle of birthing and breeding means there's not much down time for an equine veterinarian. According to a news story, a Lexington farm's chief vet said a former employee once asked him: "If you're so smart, how come you work seven days a week?" The veterinarian couldn't think of an answer.

During this trip with Newton, I find out that while he is a great admirer of Buddhism and meditates regularly, the statue in the truck is actually a fertility Buddha given to him by a Japanese client to be a guardian of broodmares. It's an appropriate talisman for the veterinarian. He joined the practice in 2000, and his first breeding season in 2001 was the season of a plague in these parts: Mare Reproductive Loss Syndrome (for more, see Chapter 14). The epidemic caused hundreds of foals to be born dead or nearly dead; countless mares aborted in early pregnancy. MRLS was linked to the mares eating the Eastern tent caterpillar, which nests in wild cherry trees and other foliage. Newton's clients lost forty foals; the economic damage to the state from all breeds was more than $300 million.

"How many caterpillars have you seen?" Newton asks the farm manager at one barn as he palpates a mare, his arm (encased in a plastic sleeve) inside the horse up to his shoulder. He pulls out the feces before he palpates, noting it is "some fine-looking guacamole."

Too many, she replies. "We are spraying the crap out of our trees — $150 a tree," she says, and at one of the far wealthier farms she saw an army of people picking nests out of branches. (The 2008 foaling season would not repeat the tragedy of 2001.)

Newton pulls his arm out. "Still Saturday," he says of the mare's breeding date, which happens to be Kentucky Derby day.

"It's all good in the 'hood," the farm manager replies, marking it on her calendar. "Are you going to the Derby?"

"Only as far as I hope to have time to watch it on TV," he replies.

After that, we look at a couple of expelled placentas that Newton drags out of two large black plastic garbage bags and throws onto the asphalt outside the barn. The placenta mirrors the lining of the uterus, so it is examined post-foaling for things such as inflammation, which could mean an infection, or missing pieces of the placenta itself, which mean parts were left in the uterus, putting the mare in danger of serious, even fatal, conditions such as laminitis. Horse placentas are T-shaped and weigh about twelve pounds each; their normal color is velvety red on the outside, shiny cellophane red on the inside.

Both placentas looked healthy and intact, but because one of the mares had bled quite a bit before, during, and after the birth, Newton told the barn manager to lavage (flush) her uterus and put her on antibiotics as a precautionary measure. It's impossible to eyeball a placenta and be certain every single piece is there, and even the smallest remnant left behind can cause big problems.

At another farm we visit a stallion Newton has known since he was sixteen — he was thirty-nine when I interviewed him. He grew

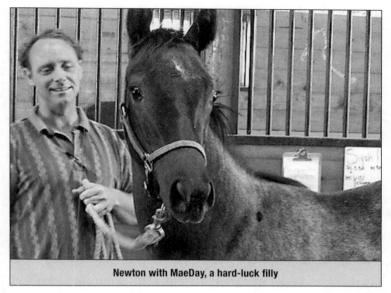

Newton with MaeDay, a hard-luck filly

up in Lexington crazy about horses and cowboys like Roy Rogers; throughout his childhood he rode, trained, and absorbed everything he could about the equine world from the broodmare farm to which his parents leased their land. In the mid-eighties, the Thoroughbred Bluegrass bubble popped (the bubble was a speculating time of astronomical prices for breeding and syndication — a stallion could be valued as much as $40 million), and the broodmare farm tanked. Newton was then around eighteen and training in Virginia for his childhood dream of competing at the Olympics in eventing, the triathlon of equine sports. He returned to Lexington and worked with his mom to turn their place into a successful boarding farm. He also gave riding lessons and kept on training for the Olympics. But he eventually decided a career as a veterinarian would be a more sensible long-term and financially fulfilling way to feed his horse obsession.

Newton first met Dr. Tom Riddle, the hospital's co-founder, and Dr. Rolf Embertson, its first surgeon, when he was fourteen years old and they came out to treat his horses for colic. "I was a nobody and they treated me like I was a somebody," says Newton. The two older vets' confidence in what they did and how they did it was also one of Newton's inspirations for going to veterinary school at Auburn. When I ask if his hours are an issue with his wife, he says she knew he was a horse addict when she married him. What is it about the horses, I then ask, that makes him an addict?

"They have an unquestioning desire to give," he says. "Horses and dogs are the only two species I know that, once they have confidence and devotion to a person, they would be willing to sacrifice everything for them."

At the next farm, I spot a dark gray filly I'd seen in the intensive care unit at the hospital. I will call her MaeDay. She was born to a twenty-four-year-old mare with fertility problems; conception had been difficult. Not long after giving birth, the mare hemorrhaged to death as a result of a uterine artery tear. A nursemare was brought in for the foal. But the nursemare, a small gray horse of mixed breeding, wouldn't bond with MaeDay or let her nurse. The newborn foal became depressed. About two days later, she got diarrhea and had to come to Rood & Riddle by herself. The diarrhea was so bad she was on the verge of dying. MaeDay had a viral infection and subsequent inflammation of the small intestine and colon. In the hospital, a second nursemare, a fawn-colored Belgian dubbed Big Mama, was brought in and fortunately bonded with the foal. After several days of care, the two went home.

Everything was fine … for five weeks. Then MaeDay got a bad fever and was found to be acutely lame in her left hind leg. Sent back to Rood & Riddle, Dr. Scott Hopper found she had a fractured sesamoid bone in her left hind fetlock. Her white cell count was high, sign of a serious infection. The filly's prognosis for recovering was poor. Yet she did. But now she has an angular limb deformity in her left hind leg; her fetlock bows in, which may keep her from racing. She'll likely be a broodmare.

In early fall, a couple months after MaeDay had gotten out of the hospital for the second time, I go out again on farm calls with Newton. One of the first farms we go to is MaeDay's home. Mist hangs over the farm's pond like Avalon. Inside a barn, chatting with the broodmare manager, we discuss the filly. Newton says she kicks. Everyone.

"She's been through too much," says the broodmare manager.

"She's a bully," says Newton.

"She's a bitch," adds Malherbe from a few feet away, scrubbing a yearling's fetlocks.

The broodmare manager nodded. She had circles under her eyes and looked resigned. "She's not even a weanling yet." When we visit MaeDay a half hour later, the filly is healthy and wary, she of light feet and suspicious eyes. I ask Newton if her trials formed her personality and he says no. "She kicked me at three days of age in my arm. For two days my arm was killing me. Finally, I realized it was because she booted me; I mean *booted*. She's tough. That's what made her live."

On this trip with the repro cowboys, by the time the first hour of the day has passed, they have: 1) blistered a yearling's front fetlocks (an irritant is injected to create swelling over the physis — growth plate — to improve the conformation for racing); 2) re-checked another yearling's corneal ulcer; 3) treated a Thoroughbred that tripped and hit his fetlocks on a fence; 4) examined a yearling for a puncture wound (the colt tried to kick the bejesus out of Newton); 5) examined a barn cat named Gordo who had an abscess in his tooth; 6) examined a Thoroughbred that ran into a fence and knocked out some front teeth; 7) treated another yearling that slipped and fell and had multiple scrapes. Afterward, Newton takes out one minute and thirty-eight seconds to run into a country store that has a sign on the front saying it sells "some hardware." He gets a ham-and-biscuit sandwich and coffee while I check out the place's arrowhead collection, located behind the supersize Reese's peanut butter cups display and the chewing tobacco. At his busiest, Newton sees seventy to 100 horses a day. (He rides on Sundays, his form of church.) When we run back to the car, I tell him he's not a slow cooker, to which the vet replies, "Microwave. Three and half minutes, high power, boiling hot. Burn your mouth."

As we drive around, Newton recounts some of his more memorable cases of late. First there was a mare I'll call Lucy, a big Australian Thoroughbred who finished in the top twenty at Rolex in 2005. She was the toughest mare her owner had ever seen. In 2008 she was impregnated with the only cryogenically frozen semen left in the world from a now-dead champion European stallion. It had been difficult getting her pregnant because she was older. She colicked about two months afterward, and it turned out a tiny hole in her cecum — the digestive "fermentation vat" between the last part of the small intestine and the beginning of the large colon — led to her death. The location of the lesion made it impossible to operate on. Newton was devastated. Right before Lucy fell ill, one of her knees was found swollen. Newton thinks she may have run into a fence, and the compression on her abdomen caused her to colic. "I tend to be very competitive," Newton says, "and the most difficult thing for me in medicine has been to accept the reality that sometimes, no matter what you do, you're not going to win. I struggle with that on a continual basis. [Lucy] reflected that struggle."

Then there was the case of Dani Girl (not her real name), a Thoroughbred mare with big eyes and a blaze, daughter of notable Bluegrass sire Kingmambo. She was purchased in Europe at a sale where she was found neglected, skinny, her feet in awful condition.

The plan was to turn her into a broodmare, hoping for offspring as fast as their father. It took a long time to get her healthy and in shape. Then, three days after being bred, she colicked. In surgery, the twist that was discovered in her intestine was so great it nearly cut off her entire blood supply. Surgeons fixed the twist, but she developed terrible diarrhea afterward, and the lining of her intestine died and sloughed off. She lost roughly 300 pounds. She was as close to dying as a horse can get. While she was recovering at the farm, Newton did a routine fertility check, assuming if Dani Girl had been pregnant before she colicked, that would no longer be the case. But she was, with twins no less. The owner had never seen a mare keep a pregnancy after colic surgery. One twin was eliminated, as is often done; it is considered difficult for a mare to carry two healthy foals to term. Dani Girl was still pregnant when this book went to press. "To survive that severe of physiological shock ... never say never," says Newton.

And who could forget the Thoroughbred weanling dubbed Bones? He had colic too severe for Newton to treat on the farm, so the vet sent him to Rood & Riddle. At the clinic, it was found he also had Salmonella, and despite aggressive treatment he was wasting away. But he wanted to live. Dr. Peter Morresey, who treated the colt at the hospital, said: "I have never seen a horse with such will." After more than $10,000 was spent on Bones' treatment, his owner, James Clay, couldn't afford to keep him at the hospital anymore and took him back to the farm of Joseph and Wendy Clay, his brother and sister-in-law, who took on the weanling's medical care. Wendy Clay massaged Bones every night in his stall, visualizing him well. The horse recovered, but was bow-legged. The farm manager said he was the crookedest horse he'd ever seen. Dr. Allen Ruggles at Rood & Riddle then did surgery designed to resolve the leg problem as the horse grew.

Some family members urged James Clay to sell Bones, saying he'd never be a racehorse. Clay wasn't sure what to do; he felt the horse's spirit was unusual and thought about naming him Ezekiel, who in the Bible brought a valley of bones to life (with God's help). He told me the following story about the night he made his decision:

"I went out to dinner, I was at P.F. Chang's, I was hanging out there with a group of people. I went to the restroom and saw a familiar face … It was [Hall of Fame trainer] Nick Zito. … I said, 'Mr. Zito, I have this horse and almost my whole family wants me to sell him, and I don't know what to do.'

"I explained the story, and after I finished talking, he pointed his finger up in the air and then pointed it to my heart. He said, 'Listen to your heart.'

"I said, 'But Mr. Zito' — and he stopped me and did it again, and said, 'Listen to your heart. That's what I do.' And he walked off."

Clay didn't sell the horse (still unnamed at this writing), his legs straightened out, and he went into training at Turfway, a racetrack in Northern Kentucky. He ruptured his tendon, however, and came back to the farm. The plan as it stood when this book went to press was to train him as a riding horse, and if he showed enough ability and his tendon looked healthy, give him one more try as a racehorse.

At another farm, I meet Newton's new intern, Dr. Erika Wierman, who has left her husband and five dogs behind in Ohio to come to Rood & Riddle for a year (and who would end up staying two). She says she's never learned so much so fast. We talk as she watches him examine a pewter-colored sport horse and listen to the owner tell him about her daughter's success on his back. Wierman, like Newton, loves this part of the job, the chitchat, the little guys. She says seasoned vets tell her, "After a while, you'll just want to make your money and go home" working for big clients. "But I'd like to think otherwise," she says to me.

When Newton is done, we get back in the car for more farm calls. Hours pass as we visit innumerable more barns. Before we had left that morning, Malherbe and I had chatted about this and that. He'd told me about his father's international fishing company, and how they zap lobsters with an electric shock so they stay prone for forty-eight hours for the trip from South Africa to their destinations. After ten hours with him and Newton, both still going strong, I am so exhausted and dazed from the pace, I realize I feel like a shocked lobster.

Newton, as noted, is a fan of cowboys, including John Wayne. The Duke's headstone reads as follows: "Tomorrow is the most important thing in life. Comes into us at midnight very clean. It's perfect when it arrives and it puts itself in our hands. It hopes we've learnt something from yesterday." But Newton lives in the moment, like a horse. Tomorrow is tomorrow. The vet says his ability to do that comes in part from meditating. Maybe that's why he doesn't lose his cool very often either. Many people don't realize the stress that comes from being a veterinarian, whether they treat small animals or large. Even if their schedules aren't as frenetic as Newton's, they deal with death five times more than human physicians, along with the worries and runaway emotions of their clients. That said, Rood & Riddle veterinarians arguably have less stress than other equine vets in more remote areas of Kentucky whose clients don't have such a hospital to go to, especially in an emergency. Those veterinarians find themselves being asked to do the impossible on the farm, or they have to euthanize a horse they believe might have been saved at a clinic. The biggest stress for Newton is that in the horse business — and at so many Bluegrass farms horses are predominantly a business — he is called at times to euthanize ailing Thoroughbreds for economic reasons, horses he would rather try to save.

As far as meditation, though, Newton learned years ago what the veterinary field is starting to recognize now: it's a power tool for navigating life's ditches and banks. A number of publications within the profession have discussed using meditation as a way to deal with stress and burnout, including the *Journal of the American Veterinary Medical Association*. It may take a while for equine veterinarians, who tend to be logic-driven workaholics, to start sitting on cushions in great numbers, but the seed is there for them to learn how to master taking things as they come as much as their patients seem to do.

When I mention to Newton that I need to start meditating again, he encourages me to do so, saying it frees you from the mental birdcage created by obsessing about the past and worrying about the future. Meditation unlitters your mind and helps you focus, he says. As we swoop into yet another green-carpeted farm, with russet-colored weanlings frolicking in the paddock like a pack of kids at recess, he says, "How many jobs do you have like this where you get to run around all day in beautiful country, be intellectually stimulated, and be paid well for it?" He's told me that before. I think he's talking not only to me but himself, marveling at his luck.

5

Divine Mare

Ten Hail Marys had been pining for a baby for three years when I met her in 2008, according to her owner, Sarah Wells, and Tammy Vosburgh, manager of the Lexington farm where the mare was boarded. The mare had torn her cervix giving birth in 2005 and had not conceived since. When spring would come and go without a birth, Ten Hail Marys would have bouts of depression, they said, standing by the fence in her paddock and staring for hours at the mares with their foals. Inside, she would press her face up to the wire mesh at the top of her stall to see the broodmare next door with her baby, even though the other mare would reach up and try to bite Ten Hail Marys to make her stop staring.

Were the owner and farm manager anthropomorphically mistaken? Is it appropriate to assume Ten Hail Marys longed for a baby the way a woman would who had been struggling with infertility? Or, was the horse's behavior real but something instinctual, divorced from personality? This leads to the debate over whether animals can have feelings as complex as ours. Wells had a filly once named Leipzig who was best friends with her half-brother.

The half-brother had to be put down because of a twisted intestine while Leipzig was at the racetrack. When the filly returned and found him gone, she whinnied across the pasture for hours. As far as other animals, in summer 2008 a group of camels, llamas, zebras, and pigs escaped a Dutch traveling circus after a giraffe kicked a hole in their cage. It's hard not to believe the breakout wasn't planned, at least a bit. On the other side of the world about a month before that, it was reported that the dogs of an older woman trapped for 196 hours following a huge earthquake in Sichuan, China, "drank rainwater, then they would lick their owner's lips to help keep her from getting too dehydrated."

Back to horses: Scientific research has found at the very least, distinct personality differences among breeds, and at the most, individual differences in personality described in human-like terms. An analysis of horse personality across eight breeds published in 2008 in the journal *Applied Animal Behavior Science* found that Arabs are anxious, excitable types; Irish draught horses mellow; and Quarter Horses "prefer to keep more to themselves." A 1998 article in the journal *Equine Clinical Behavior* noted that "The stress physiologist Herbert Weiner ... suggests 'Diseases are mere abstractions, which cannot be understood without appreciating the person that is ill.' This proposition is just as relevant to animals as it is to man. The personality of an individual is reflected in its behavior at all times, including when it is ill. Some horses respond to pain by passively withdrawing from human contact, whereas others are overtly aggressive ..."

When it came to Ten Hail Marys, however, Dr. Michelle LeBlanc, one of Rood & Riddle's reproductive specialists, was skeptical that the mare was in a human-like depression over her fertility issues. But Wells and Vosburgh were not.

Ten Hail Marys was twenty years old in 2008. She is a daughter of Halo, the famous stallion who sired Sunday Silence, who won the 1989 Derby and Preakness but flamed out in the Belmont against his rival Easy Goer. Born in 1969, Halo died in 2000; there aren't an abundance of Halo mares left.

Ten Hail Marys' dam's lines go back to Seabiscuit. She had given birth to eleven previous foals, including a Panamanian champion, Sanky Panky. She is coffee-colored; 1,200 polite, elegant pounds; friendly to people and just a little aloof to fellow horses.

Although horses these days can live into their thirties, fertility starts to decline somewhere between eighteen and twenty. But LeBlanc says fertility varies from horse to horse, dependent, as with women, on the health of the individual reproductive tract, nutrition, how well a mare handles stress, and how well she is aging. Ten Hail Marys had a major problem with her cervix, but she was both tough and even-tempered, with the spirit of a much younger horse. When I watched her gallop across the paddock one day, every movement controlled grace, she looked like an equine model out of a Bluegrass postcard. "She doesn't look like she's twenty," LeBlanc would say when she examined her. "She's aging very, very well."

In 2006, Wells asked LeBlanc, "Do we have a chance of getting pregnant again?" Wells was ready to have the cervix repaired surgically if the veterinarian, one of the world's experts on equine reproduction, thought the older broodmare could deliver a foal.

LeBlanc was doubtful. It was a "major, major" tear. "Think of a toilet paper tube and the whole top of the tube just exploded," as she put it. The vet could still insert her entire hand in the cervix when the mare wasn't in heat. But the tear was at the top of the cervix, not the bottom, which would have been much worse, almost like a gutter, allowing bacteria to flow in from the vagina. So LeBlanc replied, "Well, yeah. A chance."

"Let's try," said Wells.

Wells, who lives in Owensboro, Kentucky, is a small-time opera-tor, the kind who helps keep the horse business going with their as-pirations. She usually owns and breeds only three mares at a time. She graduated from Indiana University in 1965 and has worked as a health environmentalist in state and county government for a quarter century thus far. But what she knows and loves better than anything else are the overlooked broodmares, the ones she knows are hard-working, capable, and able to carry, foal, and raise fast sons and daughters, even if they aren't the ones you usually read about in the paper. Still you can always hope. Wells has light brown hair tossed with gray, wire-rimmed glasses, and a tendency to reel off things like Secretariat's Belmont time and decades of pedigrees, along with footnotes such as she has read documented research that proves horses cry. Ten Hail Marys was the best mare she had pedigree-wise. Wells called her a queen.

"People think everyone in horse racing is aristocratic," Wells said. "They're not. I'm a state employee. I make enough to cover expenses. The money, that's not what it's about. I don't like the rac-ing; I like the breeding. I love the babies. It's hard to let them go."

***

In 2006 Rood & Riddle surgeon Rolf Embertson repaired the tear in the mare's cervix as well as some adhesions. But he told LeBlanc what she already knew: The tear was so great he wasn't sure the mare could ever deliver a foal again. In labor, a scar doesn't stretch.

LeBlanc wished her clients realized that sometimes you have to go slow to go fast. Tissue takes time to heal. But many clients didn't listen. Wells did. She decided not to breed Ten Hail Marys for an entire year to let her cervix mend. In 2007 the horse became preg-nant with twins. LeBlanc terminated (or twin-pinched, as vets call it) one, done routinely as discussed because horses have trouble carrying twins to term. Shortly afterward, the vet found the remaining fetus hadn't made it, which also isn't uncommon.

"Do we have a chance?" Wells asked LeBlanc again.

"This mare's not going to get pregnant," the vet told her, and then relented. "OK. *A chance.*"

"Let's try again," said Wells.

LeBlanc is the last person to discourage anyone's dreams. The Michigan native went to vet school in the mid-1970s when men still greatly outnumbered women. She was one of twenty-two women out of a class of 116. Although she was putting herself through school buying young Quarter Horses and then training and selling them, her professors tried to steer her away from equine practice, believing as a woman she couldn't handle the physical demands. She was young and far more easily intimidated than she is now. In her senior year at Michigan State University in the vet school animal clinic, the male equine vets were so arrogant toward her she dropped equine and went into what's called food-animal practice — sheep, pigs, cows. Back then, she went by the nickname Micki, and when she went looking for a job after school, prospective employers were shocked when she showed up for interviews, expecting a man. Two never even came out to talk to her, leaving her in the waiting room. She eventually got into a mixed practice — food-animal and small-animal — in Maryland and then went on to work at the University of Florida in Gainesville. She had a knack for reproduction from the very start — the hands for palpating and the mind for figuring out how hormones interact.

At the University of Florida, LeBlanc invented the equine colostrometer. Colostrum is a mare's protein-packed first milk, concentrated in the last days of pregnancy; the foal suckles it within twelve to eighteen hours after birth, and it is crucial to support the baby's immune system. The colostrometer measures the milk's antibody content and tells whether the foal needs supplemental colostrum. LeBlanc went on to do more research that transformed the equine reproductive field, from the use of oxytocin (a naturally occurring hormone) to clear the reproductive tract from contamination caused by breeding (upping the odds of conception) to how to prevent placental infections in late-term mares. She left the university in 2001 to come to Rood & Riddle but continues to do research.

LeBlanc has short blonde hair and powder-blue eyes. She is fast-moving and electric. In the brief time I spent with her (she still lives in Florida part of the year) she struck me as having the iconoclastic nature that a number of inventors and scientists I have met possess: open, friendly, childlike in her enthusiasm, a Jiffy-Pop of ideas. She's an insomniac who, when she does fall into a fitful sleep, wakes up with solutions to problems in her work. To me, her presence also feels a little otherworldly. It seemed fitting when she told me her Lexington house is where the city's first airport used to be, and one of her trees shades the site of an old runway where Charles Lindbergh once landed to visit a friend. LeBlanc's not like everybody else, and Ten Hail Marys was just one more thing on which she was willing to take a chance.

***

In 2007, to the veterinarian's surprise, Ten Hail Marys got in foal again after a breeding to Birdstone, the regal-necked 2004 Belmont spoiler of Smarty Jones' Triple Crown bid and sire of 2009 upset Derby winner Mine That Bird. Every time LeBlanc came out to check on her through the pregnancy, she said, "You know this shouldn't be, but it is."

With Ten Hail Marys, LeBlanc had tried a new treatment she had been successful using with other mares. Right before the mare was bred, and shortly after, LeBlanc gave Ten Hail Marys a steroid that decreases inflammation. A normal mare can clear out the inflammation that breeding causes in the reproductive tract within eighteen hours, but a mare with problems often can't clear out dead white blood cells, which will then remain in the uterus and damage the lining.

But no matter how formidable the task, the stars (and metaphors) were aligned for Ten Hail Marys to get pregnant. She had been bred on a Sunday, in keeping with her name, and she was a last-ditch pass; time was running out and Wells knew there probably wouldn't be another game for this one.

The mare continued with the pregnancy, everyone around her nervous about the outcome. In her last trimester Ten Hail Marys received antibiotics to prevent bacterial infections, as well as other medications to block inflammation and to keep the uterus from contracting and bringing on early labor. Farm manager Vosburgh said toward the end of the mare's pregnancy, she was like any other pregnant female, human or equine — grumpy and uncomfortable. When the calcium levels in her milk finally showed she was nearing delivery, LeBlanc recommended Wells hospitalize the mare in case she needed help. Having gotten this far, the vet was worried that with all the scar tissue on her cervix, the horse wouldn't dilate easily and would stop trying to push the foal out.

"So often when they have a cervical tear … it rips when the foal starts to enter the vagina," said LeBlanc. "They stop foaling; I mean, they *just stop*. Because *it hurts*. Then, some people don't know the mare is in labor. And then you can get the placenta separating from the uterus and the foal isn't getting oxygen, and then you can have a dead foal."

Once at Rood & Riddle, Ten Hail Marys was put on what's called Foal Watch. LeBlanc thought they might have to induce labor, but induction is tricky. Foals are different from other animal babies, as well as human ones, in that their final maturation happens the last five days before birth. It is then that the enzymes needed in a foal's adrenal glands to whip up cortisol are made. Cortisol is a hormone that causes the final maturation of the intestines, lungs, metabolism, and nervous system. Without this stage, LeBlanc says, "You have a floppy foal that can't stand up." It could crush its own bones by standing on them.

The day after Ten Hail Marys arrived at the hospital, she foaled on her own, under the cover of darkness as prey animals prefer to do, ten minutes before midnight. No problems. The placenta came out on schedule afterward. Wells had had trouble sleeping that night, constantly thinking about the mare, and got the call from Dr. Peter Morresey, who was on duty, at 7 a.m.

"You've got a colt, a dark bay," he told her. "He started nursing at 2:30 a.m. and hasn't stopped since."

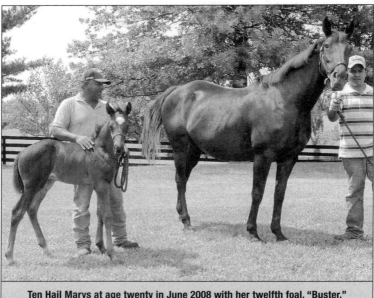

Ten Hail Marys at age twenty in June 2008 with her twelfth foal, "Buster," a few weeks after he was born

It was May, the month named after the shy Greek goddess Maia, whose name translates to "nursing mother." In Roman mythology she is a fertility goddess. LeBlanc was raised as a Catholic, but isn't religious. Still, she called the foal, nicknamed Buster, "a miracle."

Says farm manager Vosburgh: "She willed herself pregnant."

***

Wells' father was a Thoroughbred trainer; she could read *Racing Form* charts before she could words. Like a lot of horse-crazy kids, she would pretend to be a jockey on her bike. In 1995, after a lifetime in the horse business, she lost everything in the infamous Thoroughbred barn fire at Ellis Park in Henderson, Kentucky, where twenty-seven horses died. The experience was overwhelming. She got out of horses for ten years. One of the mares she lost at Ellis was by Clever Trick, the prolific stakes winner and sire of more than 600 other winners. Ten years after the fire, lured by a photo on the Web advertising the sale of a mare from Happy Trick (Clever Trick's daughter), Wells got back in the mix, buying that mare and another. When the Happy Trick mare died a couple months later of heart failure, Wells replaced her with Ten Hail Marys. Overall, Wells has been fruitful, selling one yearling for $60,000 from a mare bought for $1,900. She has been careful, shopping for mares everyone else thinks are too old, but that have terrific bloodlines. She's also unafraid of a challenge. She was the first in her family to go to college, on a full scholarship no less, graduating with honors in chemistry. In 1985, the horse that was her very first foal slipped in training on a frozen racetrack and shattered a hind pastern. Wells refused to put him down as the vet urged her to, and ten months later he was racing again. Months after I met her, after multiple conversations, she told me offhandedly that while she had been trying to get Ten Hail Marys pregnant, she had also been going through cancer treatment. "Us old girls take a while to heal," was all she would say about it.

A few weeks after Buster was born, I met her at Vosburgh Farms in Lexington. "Look at those lean and lanky legs," Wells said looking at the colt in the stall as his mother hovered over him. "He should be able to run all day with a lot of class."

Born in May, Buster was considered a "late" foal, by Thoroughbred racing standards, where everyone, as previously mentioned, wants a January or February foal. Outside the stall at Vosburgh, I commented on Buster's compact size. In addition to wanting an earlier foal, these days the trend is toward wanting a big one, believing that size makes a better racehorse. Wells replied, "For me, big is not better. It puts too much stress on the skeleton, the forelegs. As my dad used to say, 'All things being equal, a good big horse will always outrun a good little horse, but a good little horse will be around a lot longer.' "

Even though she had told me she was going to stick to breeding, as Wells stood by the stall she mulled the whole thing over, almost to herself. "Buster's a late May foal, but I may have enough guts to keep him. Now Spend a Buck (who won the 1985 Kentucky Derby) was a May foal."

Given all the talk about how much the mare had longed for a baby, I did want to know how Wells felt about ultimately taking the foal away from her and breaking up the family. "Unless you're independently wealthy," she replied, "you can't keep them as pets."

In addition, once the foal got old enough, he'd start bugging the mare when she came into heat; horses don't have the Oedipal taboo. Weaning him wasn't going to be easy, Wells added. When they weaned the mare's last baby from her, a filly, Ten Hail Marys was "a psycho wreck," said Vosburgh. The mare ran up and down the fence of her paddock for hours, dropping weight and whinnying until she was hoarse. As far as separating them, at the time Wells and I talked about it I recalled an *Equus* article from the 1980s where an animal communicator hired by the equine magazine "interviewed" the history-making racehorse John Henry. She found that years after he had been separated from his dam, John Henry still thought about her. If these things are true, I wondered: Would Buster, if sold, still think about his?

Wells, for one, thinks about her horses long after she sells them. She tracks their racing careers online and tries to find them if they disappear, worried that they might have ended up with a neglectful owner, or worse. Several months after I met her, she rescued a filly she had bred after the trainer discarded her following an injury. The filly was found in a trail riding stable; now Wells is keeping her as a broodmare. Once she ran a missing horse's picture in a southern Illinois newspaper, the way a parent would for a child. She is

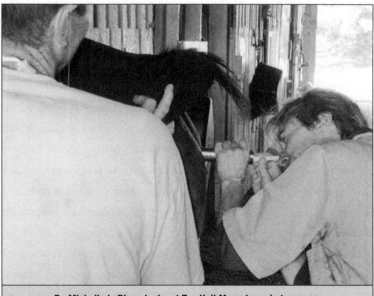

Dr. Michelle LeBlanc looks at Ten Hail Marys' cervix to assess whether the mare can get pregnant again.

still looking for a filly of Ten Hail Marys named Lilly Dale who has vanished from the racing world. Wells has called racing offices and sales companies, but her efforts have yielded no information on the horse's whereabouts.

Says Wells, "Did they turn her into a broodmare? Is she in a slaughterhouse? I have no idea and no way of finding out."

***

A couple of months passed. In August I accompanied LeBlanc on a farm call to examine Ten Hail Marys to see if it was possible for her ever to get pregnant again. The mare had torn her cervix once again with Buster's birth, but Wells wanted the final word from LeBlanc before she made the decision whether to retire the horse. It is possible for mares to carry foals to term with a torn cervix, but it depends on the extent of the damage. LeBlanc palpated the mare. Then she inserted the ultrasound.

Looking at the screen she said, "For an old mare, she's got a great uterus … there's a few cysts and a tad of fluid in the uterine body." She pulled out the ultrasound. The tech unwrapped a speculum, a silver-colored cylinder about half the size of a small poster roll, and handed it to LeBlanc. The vet inserted it inside the mare and looked through with a flashlight. "Her cervix is red, as are the walls of the cervix. Yeah, it's torn between 12:30 and 2:30 (referring to the circular entrance of the cervix)." Then LeBlanc collected fluid from the entire uterus to see if the torn cervix had adversely affected it; the fluid was clear, signifying no infection (this technique, by the way, is another process she invented). The sample would be sent to the lab for further analysis.

LeBlanc was thrilled the fluid was clear, but then said she could get three fingers through the cervix with the tear. Ten Hail Marys' tear was bigger than it was before, and I knew Wells did not want to do surgery again. I was confused by the dueling news.

Ten Hail Marys explores her new retirement home at Bethlehem Farm in Paris, Kentucky, a few minutes after being unloaded from the trailer.

I asked LeBlanc: "What's the bottom line: Are you going to recommend that she not try and breed her again?"

LeBlanc, who had been heading back to the stall, whirled around, came back, and stopped in front of me.

"I recommended that many times." Then she smiled. "Now I just give odds."

At the end of 2008, Ten Hail Marys' chances of having another foal were 10 to 1 without having surgery again, according to LeBlanc. In winter 2009, Wells retired Ten Hail Marys to Bethlehem Farm in Paris, Kentucky. Bethlehem Farm and its adjunct facility, The Center for Women in Racing, combine a retirement home for Thoroughbreds with a residential treatment program for women in the racing industry struggling with such issues as addiction and domestic violence.

Wells registered Buster with the racing name of Gatchel, after a little town in southern Indiana. As this book went to press, she was still debating whether she could afford to keep him and race him. If she does, because Gatchel was foaled in Kentucky he is eligible for purses linked to the Kentucky Breeder's Incentive Fund, and Wells has pledged any of his winnings under that state government program to Bethlehem Farm.

CHAPTER

6

Marching Orders

The large dark bay gelding was on his back, anesthetized for colic surgery. It was Sunday, April 6, 2008. Ten years earlier to the day, Marching Orders had slipped into this world, son of Captain Bodgit and Miss Stamper. Almost exactly six years earlier, he had been hurtling across the wire at Oaklawn Park in Hot Springs, Arkansas, six furlongs in 1:10:1, nabbing the winning purse of $28,500. Now, outside the operating room, nurses sheared the big country that was his stomach with electric clippers and shaved a strip down the middle with a disposable razor for the coming incision. Plastic gloves were placed on his hooves to keep the operating room sterile. Dr. Scott Hopper tucked the horse's penis inside its sheath and began suturing the sheath closed to keep urine from contaminating the surgical site. (The sutures would be removed after surgery.)

The staff was exhausted and cranky; it was late afternoon, and they had spent the day attending to nonstop emergencies after being up all night with successive emergencies.

Jennie Rhoads, the 4 p.m.-to-midnight nursing supervisor,

popped her head in the door. "That second colic got called off," she said to the surgery team.

Dr. Travis Tull, the hospital's surgical resident, looked up. "Great, so they'll be here at 2 this morning?"

"Tell them if they call back a second time it'll cost twice as much," Hopper said, finishing his suturing. He didn't mean it; he was just tired. The nurses gave the Thoroughbred's abdomen what they called a rough scrub — a first cleaning with antiseptic — followed by a sterile prep. They wheeled the horse in for surgery.

***

Marching Orders had a noble way about him. He was big and resolute; he had a paddock to himself because he played too rough. He didn't get lonely like most horses do. He talked to the occasional cow and horses across the fence, but he preferred solitude. At the Blackburn Correctional Complex's prison farm program in Lexington, the inmates called him The Viking because he would stand outside by himself through the wind and rain and cold. The only time they ever saw him go in his shed was once during a bad snowstorm.

The farm program started at Blackburn in 1999 in conjunction with the Thoroughbred Retirement Foundation, a national non-profit that saves racehorses that can no longer earn their keep, preventing them from ending up abused, abandoned, or in foreign slaughterhouses. The Blackburn program's intention is to teach inmates the skills they would need to get a job at a horse farm when they leave, as well as instill responsibility and structure, and provide a therapeutic connection to the animals. In the summer of 2008 the program had about seventy horses, ranging in age from four to twenty-six.

In March 2005, Chris Huckleby arrived at Blackburn, incarcerated on drug-related charges, and started working in the program, where each inmate is assigned an ex-racehorse to care for. He is in his mid-thirties, from Western Kentucky, with blond hair, light blue eyes, and an inmate's complexion: stark-white. He has been in and out of prison for a decade or so. He has a flatness about him, as if prison — and life — has compressed his life force. Some inmates at the minimum-security prison sign up for the farm program just for the freedom they get working in the barn, and while this was one of the Huckleby's reasons, he also grew up with horses. He understood and respected them. When he saw Marching Orders walk off the trailer, the horse fixed what Huckleby called a "spooky eye" — his right eye had white in the pupil — on him. It felt like the horse was following his every move. Huckleby begged: "Assign me that horse; I want that horse." The two became inseparable. Every time Huckleby would walk out the barn door, Marching Orders, or Mo as he was called, would run up to him. The horse would lean on Huckleby, lick him like a dog, twirl his hair with his lips.

"I don't want to sound crazy or anything, but I think this horse is trying to tell me he loves me," Huckleby told the farm manager. Horses do things like that, she replied.

Huckleby started reading books on natural horsemanship to try and decipher equine communication. He was going through a divorce and had three kids he missed. He felt like the horse knew he was having a difficult time, especially during occasions such as his children's birthdays, when Huckleby got particularly depressed. The horse would bump him with his muzzle, pull on his shirt, or play hide and seek, running behind the barn. When Huckleby came down to the barn at dusk, Marching Orders ran across the paddock to meet him. He became known as "Huck's horse." The inmate told himself and everybody else that when he was done serving time, he was going to adopt him.

***

With Marching Orders now on the operating table, Hopper stood over the horse's open abdomen. A horse's intestinal tract is seventy to ninety feet from end to end, but packed tight inside the abdomen it winds back and forth, with changes in diameter. Colic, as previously mentioned, is a broad term to describe pain caused by the intestinal tract being irritated, blocked, or bloated for any number of reasons. It is believed to be responsible for more deaths in horses than any other condition. That said, 80 to 85 percent of colics are considered "simple," and can be treated without surgery or resolve on their own. Many mild cases are what's called gas/spasmodic colic, believed to be caused by gas build-up in the colon, resulting in distension and pain. Food can also back up (from dehydration, for example) causing an impaction, which may or may not lead to surgery.

More serious cases occur when part of the large colon becomes displaced (moving out of its regular position). By doing so, a portion is subsequently shut off, like a kink in a hose, which doesn't allow the passage of food or the gas created as a normal byproduct of digestion. The large colon can also twist, cutting off blood flow. Hopper found no obvious reasons for the horse's condition in the large colon and moved on to the small colon, looking for blockage or other problems.

At Blackburn, farm program workers had found Marching Orders a few hours earlier out in the paddock trying to lie down and attempting to bite his left side, classic signs of colic. They called Linda Dyer, the farm manager, who was out of town. She was baffled when they told her the horse was colicking. Marching Orders had already been out on new spring grass for a while, and usually horses don't colic when they're used to it.

Dyer called Dr. Nick Smith, the Rood & Riddle ambulatory vet who treats the Blackburn horses. When the vet got there, the horse was down and still biting at his side, and he was in a cold sweat. His temperature was low. Smith gave him anti-inflammatories, painkillers, and other drugs hoping that would help him ride it out. But after about forty-five minutes, the horse was still in pain. Smith was worried about a rupture. He called Dyer back. "I tried to smooth him out, but he didn't smooth out," he said, recommending they transport him to the hospital.

I visited Marching Orders in his stall shortly after he had arrived at Rood & Riddle. He was covered in sweat, with pieces of hay stuck to his coat. He was heavy on his feet and lethargic. But even though he was doped up, he gave me a deep look.

Surgeon Hopper is in his forties, basketball-player tall and lean. His hair is black and gray, and he comes across as somewhat mysterious. Surgical resident Tull is a polite West Virginian, thirty years old, with glasses and walnut-brown hair with buzzed edges. He's so easygoing, you can miss how driven he is.

Once, in a conversation about the temperament of people whose work it is to slice open horses and attempt to save their lives, Dr. Rolf Embertson, a Rood & Riddle surgeon, told me how *Top Gun* is one of his and his two sons' favorite movies. They particularly like an exchange between Pete "Maverick" Mitchell (played by Tom Cruise), a pilot attending the Navy's elite school for fighter pilots, and Commander and Chief Instructor Mike "Viper" Metcalf (played by Tom Skerritt).

Viper: In case some of you are wondering who the best is, they are up here on this plaque.

(Turns to Maverick).

Viper: Do you think your name will be on that plaque?

Maverick: Yes sir.

Viper: That's pretty arrogant, considering the company you're in.

Maverick: Yes sir.

Viper: I like that in a pilot.

Said Embertson at the time, "That's kind of how I feel about surgeons." Tull and Hopper aren't as cocky as the flyboys in the movie, but they do have, as Tull put it, the confidence to "make a decision and follow through with it. No turning back."

Back on the operating table, Hopper plunged his arm in the horse's abdomen and started feeling around. After a while he said, "Oh crap," And then, "… that ultrasound doesn't tell me shit, ever."

Hopper felt around some more and then stopped. He said a phrase he often did when something wasn't right. It was from *Sesame Street*: "One of these things is not like the other."

***

From the outside, Blackburn Correctional Complex looks like a former boy's school — old-fashioned brick buildings with tall windows curved at the top — but it has always been a prison. The grounds are manicured, planted with hostas and multi-colored impatiens in spring. A small tan gazebo sits on the front lawn by the Abundant Life Chapel. The prison farm program is on 100 acres at the back end of the property. Headquarters is a converted dairy barn. It is white with green shutters, an octagonal window in the middle, and lanterns on either side. It looks like Anne of Green Gables mucks out the stalls inside, not men who have been convicted for dealing and selling drugs, DUIs with manslaughter, burglary, or writing illegal OxyContin prescriptions.

The need is great for racehorse retirement homes such as Blackburn's. In 2008, approximately 35,000 live Thoroughbred foals were reported born in North America, according to The Jockey Club. When I looked at the yearly foal report published by *The*

Blood-Horse, its blue ledgers listing name after name, it was mind-boggling to think about the competition they would face at the track. A study done by the *Thoroughbred Times* analyzing data from 1990-99 found that out of the 360,741 foals born during that nine-year period, 48.1 percent would win a race but only 3.7 percent would be stakes winners, 0.8 percent graded stakes winners. As one inmate in the Blackburn farm program told *North American Trainer* magazine in 2008, "If they were humans, they'd have their players union and they'd have their retirement package. They don't have a voice."

Dyer, who runs the Blackburn program, is a Lexington native and veteran manager of various farms in the area. She has light brown hair and blue eyes and seems chilly when you first start talking to her, but she warms up after a short while. Part of her gruffness is from being one of the only women around roughly 600 men. She teaches the inmates everything she knows: from worming and giving vaccines to how to wrap a horse's legs and feet to recognizing lameness, colic, and other problems. Because Rood & Riddle vets treat the horses, and thus have access to technology not always common outside the Bluegrass, inmates get to see things they wouldn't elsewhere — on-site digital X-rays and sinus scoping, for example.

Huckleby was one of the best horsemen Dyer had ever had. She hoped he would get a job at one of the Lexington horse farms when he got out. One of the bigger operations had hired Blackburn inmates before, with good salaries and benefits. However, challenges exist. The law is that an inmate has to get a job fourteen days after being released, and they receive bus tokens but no money for other transportation. Farms want to see you in person and looking sharp. The buses don't go out to many of the farms, numerous inmates don't have family to take them, and the clothes they are given come from Goodwill.

Huckleby was transferred to another prison in 2006 and got out in 2008. He relocated to Lexington so he could adopt Marching Orders once he saved up enough money. He had already lined up a barn where he could board him. He soon got a job with a plumbing company making a decent salary. He thought about the horse all the time. Marching Orders' previous owners, a Bluegrass couple, had acquired the Thoroughbred in a claiming race. After donating him to Blackburn, they visited the horse regularly. They were actually two of the original owners in the syndicate that bred and first raced him. When the majority of the partnership decided to drop the horse into the claiming ranks, the couple followed Marching Orders' career, and, when they could afford it, claimed him back. Huckleby had become friendly with the couple during their visits, and now wrote and called the two constantly to find out how Marching Orders was doing. When the farm Huckleby had lined up to board the horse fell through, Huckleby knew he'd find someplace else. He had to. But it had to be the right place, one where it felt safe to leave the horse.

***

In the operating room, what Hopper found was a diaphragmatic hernia — a hole in the diaphragm between the chest and the abdominal cavity — and a section of the small colon had gotten trapped inside the opening. The ultrasound hadn't picked it up because of the amount of gas distention and the hernia's location, higher on the diaphragm, more toward the horse's back. It wasn't your everyday colic.

Horses can live with diaphragmatic hernias for years (some are born with them). One cause of a hernia is trauma — getting kicked, for example. Often, diaphragmatic hernias are small, and because the lung capacity of a horse is one of the largest of all species, hors-

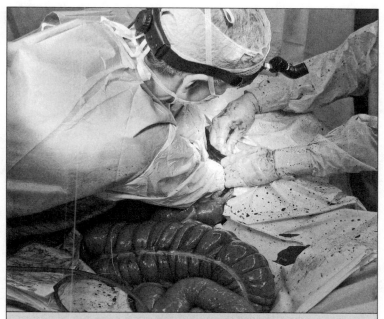

**Dr. Scott Hopper tries to suture a diaphragmatic hernia in
Marching Orders, a retired Thoroughbred from the Blackburn Correctional
Complex's prison farm program.**

es don't necessarily need all that capacity to function, especially a
horse like Marching Orders who was retired and not running on
the track.

A vet student visiting from New Zealand who was observing the
surgery asked Hopper how big the hernia was.

"Not very big," he replied, "it's fibrous," meaning it had a ring
of thick scar tissue around the edges, signifying it had likely been
there a while.

The gastrointestinal tract of a horse is not only much larger than
a person's, it moves around more. The small intestine is more mo-
bile than the small colon, so Hopper was surprised it was the latter
not the former that had, for some reason, found its way up to the
hernia that day and gotten trapped inside.

The surprise factor is one of the things Hopper actually enjoys about his work. He isn't burned out even though he's been a surgeon for more than a decade. He likes that you never truly know what's going on inside a horse until you open the animal up (kind of like a Christmas package, he told me once), and that he can take something broken and fix it.

To fix Marching Orders, the vet couldn't just pull the small colon out. The section that had gotten stuck was now bigger than the hole; that's why it had gotten stuck there to begin with. Nor could he manipulate the colon from the other side and try and milk the gas back out — the location made that impossible. He first attempted to reach deep inside the horse and expand the hernia with his finger so he could remove the colon.

The mood in the room was relaxed and a little chatty. Hopper had his left arm in the horse's abdomen up to his armpit. Somehow the conversation got off onto people whose arms were double-jointed or unusually flexible like Hopper's. Dr. Megan Romano, an intern running the anesthesia, came over for a moment and commented about how Embertson and Dr. Brett Woodie could bend some of the joints of their fingers so they looked clawed. She said she found it bizarre: "It's so gross," she added, as she stood right next to the horse's guts, with blood and feces all over the floor. Then she went back to monitoring the anesthesia.

Hopper couldn't get the hernia dilated with his fingers; he had to cut the scar tissue to widen the hole. That done, the muscle tore easily and he got the opening big enough to pull the colon out. But now the problem was trying to close the hole. The muscle comprising the diaphragm is thin, flexible, and hard to suture. Because of the hernia's location, he couldn't see what he was doing. He'd have to close by feel.

With a headlamp on even though the light added almost nothing to help guide him, Hopper plunged his left arm into the horse's abdomen up to his armpit again to draw some of the bowel and liver away from the hole; his right arm and hand followed to suture the hole closed. The curve of his right index finger shielded the point of the needle to keep it from piercing the horse's gastrointestinal tract. "There's almost no way in hell I can get to this," he muttered after about an hour. He didn't need to suture the hole completely closed — as he would with a laceration — he just needed to get enough sutures in to keep anything from going back through it. But the muscle around the opening kept splitting. Hopper kept trying. The muscle kept splitting.

Another half hour passed: "C'mon, bastard," said Hopper.

He turned back to Tull, the nurses, and visiting vets and students, "It's even more near the liver and stuff," he said of the hole. "We could leave it in there, but right now everything's running into it … and the small colon is losing blood supply." It was almost like the hernia had established a pattern now, he said, one of drawing in more of the intestinal tract.

The mood in the room had changed from relaxed to strained. For the third time, Tull made the incision in the horse's abdomen bigger to give Hopper more room. Hopper asked Romano to turn down slightly the amount of air the ventilator was pushing into the horse's lungs because lung tissue also kept returning to the rent.

Finally, Hopper said to Romano: "Go call it," to note the time of euthanization. "Goddamn," he added, mostly to himself. He asked one of the nurses to get the number at Blackburn and left the operating room without saying anything.

I walked up to the front of the table. The horse's eyes were glazed. He was missing a tooth on his right side. The room became quiet as the respirator and ventilator stopped. Tull carefully sewed up the incision.

***

On the last weekend in March, Huckleby got word his sister had been killed in a car wreck in Texas. One week later, he got a phone call at work from the head of the Thoroughbred Retirement Foundation that Marching Orders had died. The foundation knew what the horse had meant to Huckleby. After he was told what happened, it was as if the sun had been painted out of the sky. About three days after that, the wife of the couple who had donated the horse to Blackburn brought Marching Orders' halter to Huckleby, knowing he would want it. He says on that day, life became overwhelming. Depression and drinking followed and within a week he violated his parole by going out of state to Wisconsin, for family reasons, he says. As a result, he ended up back in jail, first at the Fayette County Detention Center in Lexington, in a cell where he dreamed about Marching Orders at night. Shortly afterward, he was transferred to various facilities, eventually landing in a minimum-security prison southeast of Louisville, where he was scheduled to get out in fall 2009.

Huckleby's downward trajectory had a flickering spot. One day after he got the call about Marching Orders' death, his daughter's mother called and said she'd permit him to see the child for the first time since 2004. He felt as if somehow the horse had helped him get to that point.

"The horse loved me with everything in him," says Huckleby. "He trusted me. It gave me a lot of confidence ... I wasn't loved a lot as a kid. I've been loved more by a horse than anything in my life, it's sad to say, besides my kids. He was everything to me at the time."

Vet-School Hot

So far, this book has been the story of life at an equine hospital. But what story is complete without love? In this case I am talking about vet love.

Veterinarians often marry each other. A 2007 Australian study of veterinarians found that fifteen years after veterinary school, nearly a quarter of graduates had married other vets. At Rood & Riddle, for example, surgeon Dr. Rolf Embertson is married to Dr. Claire Latimer, the hospital's specialist in veterinary ophthalmology. Dr. Scott Pierce and Dr. Debbie Spike-Pierce met at Rood & Riddle. Dr. Peter Morresey's wife works for the competition in Lexington, Hagyard Equine Medical Institute, and the spouses of Drs. Scott Hopper and Alan Ruggles both have veterinary degrees. Dr. Bonnie Barr is married to a broodmare manager, who of course isn't a vet but still knows what a red bag delivery is (premature separation of the placenta) and what needs to be done about it.

Why so much intermarriage? Is it because of the hours? Because they are the only ones who get excited about a gastro-jejunal bypass in a foal? (For non-vets, that's small intestine surgery to remove or bypass a blockage.) Successful people often say they aren't the smartest but they work the hardest. With elite vets, however, they are the smartest *and* work the hardest. Maybe it's hard to be with anyone who's not.

"Your work becomes your life," one veterinarian who is married to another told me. He said no regular person would understand his schedule: "If I'm at a dinner party, and I get a call and then say I have to go work, someone else will always say, 'You have to go to work? Now?' "

Which brings us to a discussion of vet love, at least straight vet love, in the twenty-first century. Since many people meet their future spouses in college, graduate school, or at work, this presents a challenge for female veterinarians and students. Seventy-seven percent of students in veterinary schools in 2008 were women, according to the American Association of Veterinary Medical Colleges. That's compared to 8 percent in a 1968-69 survey. The Rood & Riddle intern classes reflect the trend; in the 2007-08 class, for example, seven out of eleven interns were women; in 2008-09, eight out of eleven. As I was told by interns and externs (third- and fourth-year students who visit veterinary hospitals for up to a month as part of their program), this means a drought of available men, if you are hoping to meet one in school.

One of the interns at Rood & Riddle told me it is common in veterinary school to see an unbelievably beautiful, captivating woman with a guy who is not considered a catch, someone just not sponge-worthy. She said because of the laws of supply and demand, there is even a name for the male species of this phenomenon, considered desirable first and foremost because of his gender alone: "*vet-school hot.*"

Once, I was out on farm calls with a senior vet, a male intern, and a twenty-two-year-old female extern. The extern could have

Though love between vets can wax and wane, the love of horses remains constant.

been a Ralph Lauren model: She was a slender equestrian with long straight hair, green eyes, angel skin. When the subject came up about the roughly 8:2 ratio of women to men at her school, she nodded sadly and said, "Yeah. I didn't do too well." Another young woman veterinarian I met at one of the barns told me she looked for prospective dates in engineering classes.

One of the international interns said it is worse in Europe. She recounted one address to her class of 230 vet students, 200 of which were women. The male professor said to the men, "If you can't find a woman here, you should just forget about it."

When you ask around in veterinary circles, the easy answers for why there are so many more women over men are that men want higher salaries than veterinary jobs currently provide and that social change for women has put them into professions they didn't occupy thirty or forty years ago. But Lisa Greenhill, associate executive director for diversity for the American Association of Veterinary Medical Colleges, says there's also a more complex issue at work.

"The number of men has been on decline for years in terms of their success rate in graduating from high school and college. Vet medicine is not unique (in our attempts) to keep the men we have and attract men to the profession." Greenhill points out, however, that in academia men still make up the greatest proportion of professors and administrators. One of the key reasons is because it is difficult for women to make a tenure track since they have "additional expectations and responsibility in and outside the home."

But as far as finding love in veterinary school, Greenhill says she often hears from women students about the difficulty of it.

One of the 2008-09 interns at Rood & Riddle had a double whammy: Her brother, eleven months younger, was in the same veterinary school with her, and no male students would go near her on his watch (although as of this writing, she was, having graduated, happily dating a second-year from her alma mater).

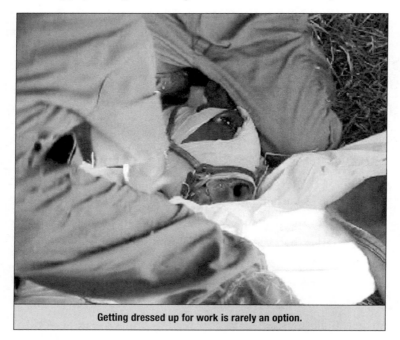

Getting dressed up for work is rarely an option.

In a related matter, female equine vets, interns, and students I met at Rood & Riddle told me it is frustrating to be in a profession where it is hard to feel pretty in your work clothes. ("I dress like a little man!" as one intern put it.) One veterinarian said they joke about writing Stacy London from the reality show *What Not to Wear* for advice. They actually know what *not* to wear but want suggestions on what they can. They can't wear low-rise jeans (try squatting down to look at a yearling's fetlocks in front of a male trio of owner, farm manager, and groom). They can't wear fabrics that stain easily, and the disinfectant mats inside the hospital's barns eat up the bottoms of their shoes. They can't wear high heels — too much grime, poop, blood, and running around. When one veterinarian told a non-vet girlfriend that she can never wear heels to work, the friend replied, shocked: *"Not even wedgies?"*

Not even wedgies.

Returning to love: It is a known fact around town that many Rood & Riddle employees, from techs to interns to veterinarians, fall in love and in like with each other, even though it is not encouraged by higher-ups. ("Don't fish in the company pond," one of the partners repeatedly says. But he's happily married. He's doesn't have to worry about a date to the Christmas party, or have to go out and get his own chicken soup when he's sick.) Some relationships last the length of a foaling season; others go on to marriage and babies. Hearts break and come back together. I looked for a love affair to write about, but I couldn't find anything quite right. The two European interns who were dating and looking for residencies near each other were shy and matter-of-fact; the two long-married veterinarians I tried to interview were close-mouthed about their lives outside the hospital's stalls. Then I realized that the reason I couldn't find anything compelling enough was because the greatest love affair going on at the hospital is between people and horses. That devotion is evident in the veterinarians who skip lunch and dinner, miss time with their young kids, and endure the silent treatment of a spouse because they want to stay at the clinic into the night trying to figure out the origin of a baffling illness (*blister beetles? yellow star thistle?*) ... or the tech who wept when recognizing that the corpse of a horse that came into the hospital to be analyzed for a study was the filly she'd cared for the previous year ... or the prominent owner of hundreds of horses who buries every single one that dies on his farm, refusing to cremate. That love never runs hot or cold.

Piaff

I nside the stall, the massive horse balanced precariously on three legs, supported by a sling around his 1,500-pound body that was suspended from a one-ton hoist in the ceiling. His name was Piaff, and he was a Dutch Warmblood gelding the color of dark chocolate. His left hind leg was too close to the right and knuckled over at the fetlock. Dr. Stephen Reed stood at Piaff's head while two interns, Dr. Niklas Drumm and Dr. Milosz Grabski, were on either side of the horse's midsection, trying to keep him standing and get the errant leg and hoof correctly positioned. Tech Josh Wilbers was also helping to stabilize the horse. Outside the stall, another tech held the control to the hoist, waiting for Reed's direction to start moving it up and down.

Piaff's owner suspected he had wobbler syndrome. Specific nerves permit a horse to sense its limbs; the syndrome develops when a compressed spinal cord damages or kills these nerves (resulting in a wobbly gait). Piaff had had neurological problems for more than a year and a half now, and, despite various treatments, he was still ill. He had just been driven down from the University of

Wisconsin's veterinary teaching hospital to Rood & Riddle, where Reed is one of the world's experts in equine neurology. It had been a ten-hour trip, and Piaff had lain on his side the whole way. He had tried to get up several times when the owner stopped to check on him, but he was too weak. It's not good for a horse to be down that long; they can't take full, deep breaths, or eat, drink, urinate, or defecate normally. It took about ten hospital staff members to get him out of the trailer, with Piaff sedated and pulled on the glide.

Everyone in Piaff's stall was tense. "Get a bucket of water," said Reed to someone standing by the door. "Something normal, something he might relate to. He's kind of trying to move his lips. I don't think he's awake just yet." Water was fetched, but Piaff wouldn't drink.

"We have to look out for his hind legs," Reed said. "If they're caught underneath, he'll go back down." The vet gave the go-ahead, and tech Megan Howard started raising and lowering the hoist again in tiny increments. But soon, Piaff's legs started to crumple and the horse began to spin around.

"Stop, STOP!" yelled Reed, walking toward Piaff's left side. The vet's head came up to the horse's back. Howard stopped the hoist. "Down, just a mite," said Reed; she complied. "Let him balance, guys!" Reed said to the interns and Wilbers. "I don't mean to be so bossy," he added, and everyone assured him it was OK. They knew he was just worried about the horse getting injured.

Piaff steadied himself on three legs again. His left hind leg was now in a better position for stability, but it was still knuckled over. He swayed. Wilbers and Grabski reached out to help him.

"Wait just a little bit; let him see if he can do it," Reed said. "Let him have his head. He needs to feel like he's in control."

By now, it was around midnight. It was cold outside, just below freezing. The double doors at one end of the barn were open because Piaff's trailer was still backed up to the entrance, and when the wind blew through it felt 10 degrees colder. Hay dust was everywhere; it got in your eyes and throat. It had been about two and a half hours since Piaff was unloaded from the trailer. In addition to the hospital staff members helping Reed, a small crowd of techs and barn crew had gathered outside the stall to watch and help if needed. Everyone was shivering and tired … except for Reed. He was at least twenty-five years older than most of the people present, yet, as usual, even after a sixteen-hour workday, the vet was bouncing around like a superball, clad in a black-and-red Gore-Tex jacket.

Piaff tentatively picked up his left hind leg and put his hoof flat on the floor. His legs trembled.

"I think he's tired," said a tech.

"I think if he goes back down we're in big trouble," said Reed.

"He's slipping here," said Wilbers.

"Can someone go get his bloodwork?" asked Reed.

Piaff leaned back and then caught himself with his hind legs, the red hoist rolling on small wheels across the ledges of the steel beam stretching over the stall. The horse leaned his backside against the wall to balance.

"C'mon," said Reed encouragingly, "use it like a fifth wheel."

The horse rolled back and forth a bit and then righted himself without the wall. The sound the wheels made when they rolled was like a bowling ball traveling down a lane. "That'll be good," said Reed.

Drumm was now in front of the horse. Piaff leaned in and put his head against the intern's chest. Drumm put his hand on the horse's head. Everyone relaxed, especially the owner, who knew Piaff didn't trust just anybody. In a few minutes, she needed to drive eight hours back to Chicago for medical school, and now felt a little more comfortable leaving him.

Reed came out of the stall and conferred with her about his plans for the following day. The vet said that if Piaff's myelogram — a special X-ray of the spinal canal that reveals cervical compression — showed he was a wobbler, the horse would go immediately to surgery. The owner nodded, exhausted. Reed continued. "Right now, we'll give him some hay, shut the lights, and let him relax. Someone will be with him all night."

***

It is not uncommon for veterinary students to refer to Dr. Stephen Reed as "a god" although he bats away compliments and defers credit for furthering his field to others. However, Reed co-edited the seminal text on equine neurology and conceptualized and co-wrote the handbook *Equine Internal Medicine*, first published in 1998. It is the only internal medicine textbook focused solely on horses. Reed is a retired professor in equine medicine from Ohio State University, about six feet tall, with bristly gray hair and wire-rimmed glasses. He is the first to admit he needs to step up his time at the gym. The vet has the brain of a major league scientist and the ebullience and goodwill of the Cookie Monster. For years he had a piece of paper taped to his computer that read: "No one cares how much you know until they know how much you care." Clients love him for that. At the veterinary hospital, he tends to jump from one thing to another, with staff members trying to keep up with him, or find him.

Reed has been drawn to horses since he was a kid growing up in Ohio. When the circus came to town, he would hang out with the performers and their three-ring ponies. (His mother didn't like it, thinking the big top wasn't a wholesome influence.) In high school he got to spend more time with horses helping a friend's busy veterinarian father. In veterinary school at Ohio State, a professor, Dr.

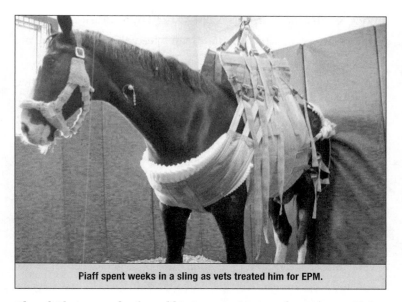

Piaff spent weeks in a sling as vets treated him for EPM.

Cheryl Chrisman, furthered his interest in neurology, demystifying the brain and paths to diagnosis.

In his work, one of Reed's favorite sayings is, "This horse wants to live." The phrase is framed and hanging on a wall in his office. It's also the caption underneath the caricature of a rattled, upside-down horse drawn for him by a colleague's wife.

The morning after Piaff arrived at Rood & Riddle, I caught up with Reed early while he was doing a myelogram on another horse. I asked him if he had a sense of what the warmblood's problem might be. "She's going to have to make some serious decisions," he said of the owner. "I don't think his spine is compressed. There's too much muscle atrophy. It could be EPM, disuse, or Lou Gehrig's disease (referring to equine motor neuron disease)." The horse, who was eleven years old, had been diagnosed about a year and a half earlier with equine protozoal myeloencephalitis, or EPM, an infection of a horse's central nervous system.

EPM is the most commonly diagnosed neurological disease

among North American horses. It is caused by a parasite contained in opossum feces, which contaminates feed that a horse unwittingly eats, along with drinking water. One of the problems with EPM is that it can be difficult to diagnose; it can look like other neurological diseases; symptoms can be mild incoordination or weakness so severe a horse can't get up. Yet one distinctive sign is asymmetry in the presentation of symptoms, such as the abnormal gait Piaff exhibited.

In the beginning, Piaff had undergone treatment for EPM for four months and improved, but when the treatment was discontinued, he started to have problems again, including ones different than before, such as extreme muscle wasting in his hindquarters.

Veterinarians thought Piaff might need larger doses of EPM medication because of his size. But that didn't work, and despite the horse seeing multiple veterinarians over several months, the owner could not get a diagnosis she thought was accurate. She had previously experienced success using colloidal silver, an alternative treatment some people consider a disease-fighting agent, and tried it again. Piaff began to improve, but neurological symptoms showed up again a couple months later and continued for about a year. Two different tests for EPM showed he did not have the infection, and Piaff came to Rood & Riddle after a week at the University of Wisconsin, where he was not responding to treatment for "neurologic disease, unknown etiology."

For Reed, it would actually be good news if Piaff's spine showed compression because then at least a clear treatment path existed: "basket" surgery or cervical stabilization. The vertebrae are fused with a metal implant (the "basket").

A few hours later Reed performed the myelogram on Piaff. The gelding was anesthetized and his head placed on a small ramp to keep the dye that was then injected through a spinal tap from going into his brain. (Cerebrospinal fluid was also taken for analysis.) On the X-rays the dye would show any lesions compressing the spinal cord. Radiographs of the horse's spine were then shot in nine different positions. If Piaff had a compressed spine, he would, as Reed had told the owner the night before, go straight to surgery because of the severity of the case. The operating room was already being prepared.

The techs quickly developed the X-rays. When Reed examined them, he didn't see compression anywhere on Piaff's spine. Frustration. Dr. Brett Woodie came into the radiology suite; he would be the lead surgeon on the operation, with Reed assisting.

A small commotion followed Woodie into radiology; his tech had just been injured and staff members crowded around him wanting to know what had happened. Woodie had just finished what's called a dynamic exam on a Thoroughbred's airway. During the exam the horse exercises on a high-speed treadmill while its upper airway is evaluated through an endoscope. Despite taking all safety precautions, the horse had kicked Woodie's tech.

"We heard a scream and she was down on the ground," Woodie told the vets and techs in the small radiology room. He said it looked like "her wrist was *hanging*." But after her forearm and wrist were examined and iced, the tech turned out to be physically OK, just shaken up. Most non-horse people don't think much about the dangers of working with large animals. Accidents aren't common, but they happen.

Reed handed the X-rays to Woodie, who clipped the first set to the light stand. "This layer's all good," he said. Woodie didn't see any compression on the second set either. He and Reed were in agreement.

"I'll tell surgery he's a no-go for a basket," said Reed.

Reed was worried. Options were limited if they, too, couldn't diagnose Piaff. At Wisconsin, Piaff had also been in a sling, unable to walk on his own. Horses can't use wheelchairs. How long could Piaff last if nothing was found soon to get him better? The night before, Reed had encouraged the owner to say her good-byes to the horse before she left, in case he had to be put down. She wouldn't do it.

Piaff, still sedated from the test, was taken back to his stall — via the glide pulled by a mini all-terrain vehicle. There, Dr. Travis Tull was set to do a muscle biopsy, which would tell whether Piaff had equine motor neuron disease. It would take a week to get the results.

Dr. Lori Bidwell monitored Piaff's depth of anesthesia as Tull did the biopsy. While assessing the horse, she asked the interns and techs in the stall to form an analysis on what they thought the horse's problem might be. The answers included: herpes, West Nile virus, rabies, motor neuron disease, and again, EPM.

Blood dripped onto the white square of gauze that an intern held for Tull. He extracted a tiny piece of muscle from the area to the left of the base of Piaff's tail, placing it on the gauze.

Everyone in the stall was glum, worried about the warmblood.

Before Piaff got sick, his charisma struck nearly everyone who saw him.

Trying to lighten things up, Bidwell recalled a horse named Juju that had had West Nile virus while she was at Michigan State, where she did her residency in anesthesia. "She spent eleven days in a sling and came out of it," she said. "There's hope." Nobody in the room looked hopeful.

Reed came back from a phone call with Piaff's owner. "She's come to the decision she needs a couple more days. She wants to say goodbye. I told her if he struggles and starts thrashing around, we'll let her know. Otherwise, we'll manage him until the weekend."

***

Piaff's owner (who prefers to be anonymous) had bought him in The Netherlands in the fall of 2002 as a dressage horse. When he first came to the United States, the horse was a nervous wreck. Everything stressed him out, from his neck being touched to the sight of the dust mop used to clean the rafters of his stall. His owner didn't know how he was previously treated, but it didn't appear to be well. It took a long time for them to develop an unspoken communication. With patience, he relaxed, becoming more trusting, less anxious. From working with him, the owner learned the importance of standing back and observing a challenging situation, be it with a horse or a person, and to look for underlying reasons for why things had gotten tangled up. Both species usually have a reason for acting the way they do, and, "The first assumption should be that they're not doing anything on purpose to make your life difficult," she told me. She did not ride Piaff in competitions, preferring instead to participate in dressage clinics.

Piaff was striking to everyone who saw him — his size, the shimmer of his coat, the lightning bolt blaze down his face. As he matured and calmed down, becoming more expressive and communicative, people were drawn to him even more. It was true animal magnetism. Bicycle riders and walkers near one farm where he was boarded used to stop when they saw him. They couldn't resist coming up to introduce themselves and beg for a nuzzle.

Back at Rood & Riddle, after the myelogram, Piaff could not get up for seven and a half hours. The stress of the trip from Wisconsin, the anesthesia from the procedure, and whatever disease he was suffering from had left him too weak to move. The owner came back down to Rood & Riddle from Chicago. When she saw how weak he was, she thought, "OK, we're done." But then, some light. The cerebrospinal fluid taken at the beginning of the myelogram showed he was positive for antibodies against the parasite, *Sarcocystis neurona*, which causes EPM. Now, Reed had a treatment course.

EPM testing is thorny; no test exists that can tell, with 100 percent accuracy, if a horse has the disease. The neural tissue that *S. neurona* invades can't be taken from a living horse. (The only 100 percent accurate test for EPM, as Reed and other veterinarians say, is a postmortem.) So the three major EPM tests, which all use different approaches, look for antibodies *against* the parasite, circulating in the blood and/or cerebrospinal fluid, as evidence of the infection.

Piaff's last two EPM tests, done a month or so before, had indicated he did not have the disease. Both were done using blood samples. The owner thought perhaps the September tests had been inaccurate. It can happen. Or, maybe he didn't have a measurable antibody level at the time of the previous tests, another scenario. Testing the cerebrospinal fluid is considered the best way to diagnose EPM, and the owner now wished she had requested that at the start. She hadn't because he was already being treated for EPM anyway and she was advised, correctly, that blood contamination during a spinal tap can sometimes render a false result. As time went on and Piaff relapsed, she didn't know if he had a continuing disease and what it was, or if he had worsening nervous system damage from EPM, despite therapy.

In the end, whichever test (or combination of tests) is chosen is a matter of preference, for the client and the veterinarian, and has to be evaluated in combination with clinical signs and by ruling out other diseases and conditions. Reed prefers a test called the Western blot; his research contributed to its creation. (The Western blot works by detecting antibodies against different proteins from *S. neurona*, giving a positive or negative result rather than a level of concentration.) For Reed, everything in Piaff's case added up to EPM.

At Rood & Riddle, Piaff immediately began aggressive treatment for EPM. By the next afternoon, he was back up in the sling when I came by his stall. He looked alert and happy, bouncing back, Reed thought, from the stress of the past two days and the anesthetic clearing out of his system, and benefiting from the anti-inflammatories used as part of the treatment. Piaff was not leaning against the wall for support.

The owner was tweaking the hoist at Reed's direction. "I can't believe he's standing like that," she said.

"He seems to know this (sling) will help him and we're there for him," said Reed. "Now, he's relaxing into it."

A tech took his temperature. It was normal.

***

Although the disease that was later to be called EPM was first recognized in the 1960s, it took about thirty years to figure out that the opossum is what's called the definitive host, and the only known one, of the parasite, *S. neurona*, which causes 90 percent of EPM cases. Inside a definitive host, a parasite matures and reproduces. Opossums walk up to a half-mile a night, can live almost anywhere, and eat anything (as anyone with a cat door knows).

They have litters twice a year. All this means these scavengers can spread EPM like crazy after eating an intermediate host, which carries cysts of *S. neurona* in its muscles. The intermediate hosts identified so far include skunks, raccoons, armadillos, cats, even the sea otter. The infection then passes through the opossum into its stool, which can contaminate horse feed and water sources. The horse is a dead-end host for *S. neurona*, meaning the parasite's life cycle comes to an end in the horse. Unfortunately, however, in a twist of biology, *S. neurona* is stubborn and can multiply without reproducing (the way cells can divide), causing more central nervous system damage.

Piaff's owner thought he might have gotten EPM at one of the first barns where he was boarded after being imported from Europe. Other horses there had the infection. Horses can't catch EPM from each other, but *S. neurona* might have been lurking in the feed and water.

Since EPM first appeared, numerous people have contributed to breakthroughs in fighting the disease, working long days and late nights in their offices and labs, and out in the field. Reed has been part of that research effort; his work and that of colleagues has led to such steps as identifying the cat as an intermediate host and helping to figure out the life cycle of *S. neurona*. He's also helped bring new drugs to market and develop a vaccine. The vaccine hasn't worked, but the research in creating it has brought forward new, essential information.

When Piaff had first become ill, his owner had talked by phone to Dr. Peter Morresey at Rood & Riddle. To Morresey, it all sounded like EPM. The owner called the vet regularly for advice as the medical journey unfolded.

"Swing for the fences," Morresey would tell her. "As long as the horse wants to live, go as hard as you can. Swing for the fences."

Morresey has been down the EPM road with many patients. Some responded immediately to treatment, recovered, and were ultimately fine, especially if the infection was caught early. Others got better, but then relapsed multiple times. A number of horses got better but the spinal cord had been scarred and they were never as strong as before. As Morresey puts it, "The spinal cord doesn't like to be pissed off," because it has a limited ability to repair itself.

Many factors contribute to a fair to bad outcome for horses diagnosed with EPM: the level of absorption of medication, how it is distributed in the nervous system, the innate ability of a particular horse's immune system to respond, and other variables. Morresey told me the central nervous system is a difficult place to treat because it's hard to get drugs to successfully cross the blood-brain barrier.

Over the next few days Piaff improved. In addition to the EPM medication and other treatment such as antibiotics, he was getting two medications to boost his immune system, along with vitamin E, acting as an antioxidant. He learned how to use the hoist even more skillfully and didn't strain his neck against the sling like some horses do. A big piece of foam was placed between his chest and the sling to help prevent pressure sores. Pine bedding was put on the stall floor instead of straw to give him more traction and prevent slipping. Not every horse will stay in a sling without panicking. Some will thrash, unable to overcome their genetic desire for flight when feeling trapped. But despite being so constrained, Piaff was calm, alert, accommodating, *bright*, the kind of patient everybody likes to be around. His left front leg, which had been swollen when he arrived, started to improve with hydrotherapy and other treatment. Yet his penile sheath, which had also been swollen upon arrival, remained so. Techs were with him virtually twenty-four hours, feeding him fresh grass they handpicked outside the barn, along with carrots and horse cookies called Meadow Mints his owner had left for him. Piaff was also fun; he liked to butt his caregivers gently. Almost no horse likes to be alone, and Piaff was no exception. He was becoming close to the people around him, and they to him.

"He's a fighter," said tech Julie Mercado when I visited one afternoon. "That's what's helping him right now. His will. He wants to get better."

But although he was improving, Piaff was not getting the deep sleep he needed standing in a sling. By Thursday of his first week at Rood & Riddle, he had not lain down to sleep since he had arrived. When his legs buckled underneath him, Reed let him stay down and sleep for two and a half hours. But he couldn't stay down too long; he'd be vulnerable to pneumonia and other problems. The hoist was used to get him back up. The next day, Piaff was sparky again, having had some rest. He seemed to be standing on his own, even with the sling on. In the midafternoon Reed came to check on him. Nursing supervisor Kirsty Nolan was on watch.

"We have to establish a plan to get him out of the sling and out of the hospital," said Reed to Nolan. "If we could just get him to start moving. I think even if he just steps around it would be good for him … to get his coordination improved, his strength improved."

Piaff stood looking at the vet. He was starting to get a pressure sore from the sling on his right hindquarter.

"It seems like he's holding himself up," the vet continued. He loosened the straps of the sling a little and then had Nolan move the hoist down so Piaff could bear more weight, yet still be supported by the sling if he needed it.

"He's so unsure of himself and lacks confidence," said Reed.

"They learn to compensate," Nolan said.

I asked Reed if Piaff had become psychologically dependent on the sling. "That's personifying," he said, "but that's what I think. I'd like to see him walk in a circle." He slapped Piaff on the butt lightly. Piaff stepped around tentatively and stopped. "That's it. C'mon. C'mon. See, it's much stronger," the vet said of the swollen left front leg.

The vet kept urging the horse to walk. Piaff reluctantly moved around in a circle.

"My goal is to have him out of the sling by the weekend," said Reed. "The week after that, a lay-up farm. We need an endpoint for this client ... I think Piaff is stronger today. If he was in an arena, I bet he'd walk without falling."

For the third time, Reed was able to get Piaff to make a slow circle in the stall.

Earlier in the day, Danielle Thomson, an internal medicine tech, had stopped by to see how Piaff was doing. Thomson had worked briefly as a nurse in a regular hospital. After about eight months, she came back to equines. The money was better treating people, but one of the reasons she left was that it was too painful to be around people suffering at the end of their lives. Horses could be euthanized.

When Thomson was working with people, she had seen patients who were afraid to get out of bed after a serious accident such as breaking a hip. After a point, it was psychological.

"You have to make them get out of bed," she told me. "You have to say, 'I will be there for you. I will catch you if you fall. I won't let you fall.' " After visiting Piaff, she also believed the horse might be afraid, clinging to the sling for security.

Back in Piaff's stall, Nolan did some physical therapy on his left front leg, lifting and stretching it. He was stronger than he was the day before.

***

One of Rood & Riddle's receptionists, Chris Pfetzer, has a son, Mark, who in 1996 at sixteen was the youngest person to climb Mount Everest. During the expedition, eight climbers died in a storm. Mark reached the highest camp, but not the top. While I was writing this book, Chris lent me her son's book about his teenage years climbing and summiting the world's highest peaks. One of its passages reminded me of Piaff's case:

"Routes are not all precise. They deal with broad areas. You might aim for a particular rock face or gully, which leads you to a ridge you have to cross. You have to consider the location of camps, too, because they offer safety, protection. But no matter how well you plan a route, you never know what's ahead of you … "

Toward the end of Piaff's second week in the hospital, he was taken out of the sling for the first time. He stood on his own for twenty minutes, but then, twitching flies away with his tail, lost his balance and fell. A pressure sore was developing on his left hip and another in the accompanying axillary region (armpit), which worsened after he was hoisted back up in the sling. Two days later, he swung across the stall again via the hoist and lost his balance, although he was able to regain it on his own.

By the third week, despite treatment and padding, the pressure sores worsened, the one under his armpit draining pus. It was swollen and sensitive to touch. Piaff started leaning his left side more and more against the wall. The left front leg was still being treated regularly, but the swelling had stopped going down, and the leg had gotten stiff. The edema in his sheath increased. Piaff was getting weaker.

"I'm just so upset," said Reed, when I caught up with him. "I can't get that wound to heal in the axillary region … and he needs to learn to go to sleep and get some long sleeps. Horses need to sleep, just like people. You can't heal if you don't sleep, you know?"

Although Piaff was still sunny most of the time, he started to have moments of depression — sometimes he wouldn't nicker at the prospect of a treat or would lose interest while being petted. It seemed as if Piaff might be sliding down a mountain. Yet he didn't want to die.

***

Piaff continued to decline. By the end of the third week, nobody who worked in the hospital could remember a horse ever being in a sling that long. Meanwhile, the owner had been reading about the human drug interferon and how it stimulates macrophage response in people. Macrophages are large white blood cells that have an important role in initiating immune system response (among other things). She also read that interferon activates the responsiveness of natural killer cells, another important player in the immune system.

Interferons are natural chemical messengers in the body (from a larger group of proteins called cytokines) produced by cells infected with a virus or cancer. The messengers "interfere" with the replication of a foreign pathogen, before it develops antibodies, and also stimulate the immune system. Depending on their molecular structure, most interferons are classified as alpha, beta, or gamma. The different forms have different roles. Interferon medication mimics naturally occurring interferon.

The owner had also read various veterinary studies, including one that showed mice that were genetically developed to have part of their immune system knocked out — the part containing interferon gamma — were more susceptible to parasitic and protozoal diseases, and EPM is such a disease. Interferon gamma helps regulate the immune system. She asked Reed: If the interferon level in

Piaff was increased, could that possibly boost his immune system and fight EPM?

Reed was hesitant. An experiment in a mouse might not apply to a horse. He had never used interferon for EPM, didn't know of any case that had, and wasn't sure what the dosage should be. Also, interferon gamma wasn't available to him as a pharmaceutical, only a form of interferon alpha used to fight some types of leukemia, skin cancer, hepatitis B and C, and other diseases. Reed was also concerned that Piaff was starting to truly suffer. Yet he wanted to save the horse as much as the owner. *This horse wants to live.* He thought there was a shot the interferon could turn on immune-fighting cells, including those that produced interferon gamma. He said he'd try the drug for a week or so, which is about how long it would take to show any impact. But if Piaff showed no improvement, Reed thought the horse should be euthanized. The owner was relieved the vet was willing to try.

The interferon was ordered Friday, but couldn't arrive until Saturday. I found Reed in the admissions building Saturday morning waiting for the medication. It was supposed to be there by 10:30 a.m. and wasn't. He was upset. "The client is looking at me expecting me to do something," he said. "I'm really discouraged." He went down to the barn to check on the horse. The winter's first snow had come the night before, and the rooftops of the light brown barns were frosted; they looked like gingerbread barns. The cold was bullying.

In the barn Piaff leaned against the wall. He looked like a war victim. The pressure sore on his right hindquarter was bigger, the skin now gray and flaking off. His right hoof was in what's called a soft ride boot for support because of concerns about laminitis — he was leaning on his left side too much, putting little weight on the right. The pressure sore under his armpit now looked like a shark bite; occasionally he tried to lick it. He was having respiratory problems. The night before I had read a magazine article about the rise in America's fondness for pets. It said the French call their dogs *bêtes de chagrin* — beasts of sorrow, recognizing that to love a dog is eventually to mourn it. To my eyes, Piaff seemed to be turning into a horse of sorrow.

Reed needed to leave. He had promised his wife and out-of-town family that he'd spend time with them that weekend, actually since Thursday, and had barely done it. Like many veterinarians, he was in trouble with the ones he loved over his work schedule. He'd have his intern, Dr. Birthe Pegel, give the horse the medication when it came. But just as he was driving out, he got a call from the pharmacy that the interferon had arrived.

Pegel jumped in Reed's car to stay warm after he phoned her from the parking lot, and they discussed the dosage. The small

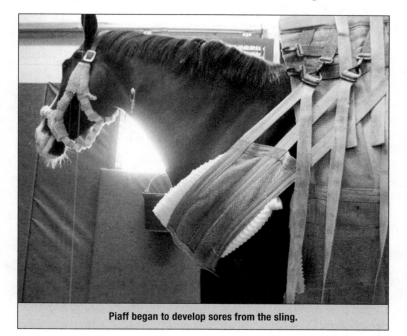

Piaff began to develop sores from the sling.

Styrofoam cooler with the orange sticker that read "SATURDAY" on the top contained 20 million units of Interferon alfa-2b, divided into two doses. Reed decided they should give Piaff a half dose Saturday and a half Sunday and see how he fared. He drove Pegel down to the barn. It had started to snow.

After preparing the medication in the small office in Piaff's barn, Pegel went into the stall where the horse leaned against the padded wall: "Hi, Piaff. I need your neck. You like your wall, I know. Just let me give it to you." Piaff licked his lips and put his muzzle over her shoulder as she injected the drug into his IV catheter. "That's it," she said.

As she left, Pegel said, "I think he's getting weaker." We talked briefly about whether she thought he should be euthanized. She was nonjudgmental about the owner's desire to keep trying: "Everyone's different about how long they hold on to their horses."

Pegel had never given interferon to a horse, but she had worked her way through veterinary school manning a pharmaceutical hot line for human multiple sclerosis patients using the drug. Patients who called in had side effects such as fevers, chills, muscle aches, and headaches. For people who used the drug a long time, skin problems often developed near the injection sites.

Back in the office, Pegel read off the side effects from the safety material: "flu-like symptoms, skin problems … blood sugar problems …" More than fifty different potential side effects were listed. Neither Reed nor she thought the interferon would hurt Piaff at this stage, but they did not truly know what side effects might occur. Reed was more worried about the drug having no impact.

Pegel went to check on Piaff one more time before she left. "Don't lick your wound," she told him.

Despite all his problems, Piaff was still bright. He hadn't gone dead behind the eyes, as Ryan Nesemeier, the tech who was caring for him that day, put it. The contrast was as incongruous as the crimson roses still blooming outside the hospital admissions building in the middle of the falling snow.

***

The next day, Piaff seemed roughly the same, although one of the techs thought he might have improved a bit. But after Wednesday, he kept going downhill. He didn't seem to be having any side effects from the interferon, but it also didn't appear to be helping. On Friday, he stood up for eight minutes on his own without the sling and then collapsed. By now, it was the weekend before Thanksgiving, four weeks since Piaff had arrived at Rood & Riddle. I left to see family out of state. On Monday I called from the Northwest; Piaff had been put down that night, the owner's decision. The necropsy showed EPM was what Piaff indeed had. His spinal cord showed substantial lesions containing *S. neurona*. A postmortem that reveals a horse had EPM will usually show the identifiable trail *S. neurona* leaves behind in damaged tissue, but it is actually unusual to find the organism itself.

The owner's love for Piaff went so deep she couldn't find the bottom. She was struck by his character. During the entire medical experience, he never once pinned his ears back toward anyone (a sign of anger or feeling threatened), even when he woke up in Wisconsin in a sling for the first time. "He knew people wanted to help him." She repeatedly went over the course of his illness in her head. She wondered if the colloidal silver might have undercut the effects of the earlier EPM medication, as well as if the right drugs had been given to him early on … or if something in Piaff's immune system had made him unresponsive to them. She felt she had failed her horse. Reed didn't know the answers and thought probably nobody would. But he thought it was natural to question choices in a complex medical crisis. The owner said one of her biggest lessons was that "neurological illness should not be left up to an average vet. Get the horse on a trailer and take him to a specialist (no matter how far away). You don't have time. You need a quick, definitive diagnosis. Every day you miss is a day where more damage is done."

When I emailed with her four months later in spring, she wrote of the loss, "It is still very raw. I still can't believe he is gone. I cannot really grasp that he is gone. When I stop to think about it, it is still very painful." Her email reminded me of what a veterinarian and veterinary scholar I interviewed once told me a client said about losing a pet: It was like a color was missing from her life. The color of Piaff was gone, and it would be a long time before the owner stopped being aware of it.

Selena

"The horizon is the edge of your polo field, the earth is the ball in the curve of your polo stick. Until you are blotted out of existence as the dust, gallop and press on your horse, for the ground is yours."
— Twelfth-century Persian poet Nizami's advice on how to live a full life

Picture the college sophomore: She is slender, long black hair, green eyes, a face that belongs on a Roman coin. It is late January. Mia Proto is beat; she played six chukkers (seven-minute periods) of polo, round-robin style, last night at the Kentucky Horse Park on the University of Kentucky polo team. In her calculus class she gets a text message from the farm where her horse, Selena, is boarded. It says to call right away, it's about her horse, the vet is coming. Proto runs out of class and speeds to the barn in her old blue Volvo.

Picture the horse: The day before, Selena's dark bay coat shone in the arena, all 880 pounds of her doing exactly what Proto wanted in this hockey game on horseback. She held ponies twice her size off the line, galloping full-throttle the length of the arena and stopping five feet from the wall. Proto played Selena again for the third chukker instead of the normal two periods per pony because there weren't any fresh horses, but Selena was fit enough. Now at the barn, as Proto looks at Selena, it's an unbearable sight. Her eyeball appears to be hanging out of her left socket; it's a red, jelly-like blob. Her left hind leg, haphazardly bandaged with someone's T-shirt, has one severe laceration down to the cannon bone, along with a couple of smaller ones. Her head and neck are so swollen she can barely hold her head up or breathe; the swelling is blocking her airway. Selena looks like a crime victim. The people at the farm say she ran through a fence.

Picture the night before in the pasture: You can't. Humans know very little about what goes on at night between horses. During the day, they look so peaceful out there … that is not always true. In many pastures, rivalries and competition are everywhere, especially when horses are thrown together at boarding facilities. (With bands in the wild, however, that's usually not the case, save for stallions vying for a mare.)

Proto asks me: Do you ever notice how they're grazing and roaming in different corners, some alone, some bunched together? Those are cliques, she says. "Once the pecking order is established with horses," Proto says, "very rarely does a high-ranked horse get marked down. It's kind of like working in an office." But the equine version can get brutal. Once, Proto and her team loaded three horses, Salsa, Secta, and Rosa, into a trailer for a match, and when they were unloaded at their destination one of Secta's ears was torn off. Teeth marks showed in its place. Rosa, known for possessing a bad attitude and a mean streak, remains the prime suspect. Even Selena, quiet, a little standoffish, something of a loner, isn't immune to taunting. Back at Proto's family's farm in Slaterville Springs, New York, Proto watched one afternoon as Selena challenged another horse she knew she could beat to a race and did. But down here in Lexington, at a strange farm away from home, Selena is submissive, one of the lowest on the totem pole. She is the type of horse, according to Proto, who "needs a human next to her to make her feel strong. Someone to protect her. But she also needs someone she can push against."

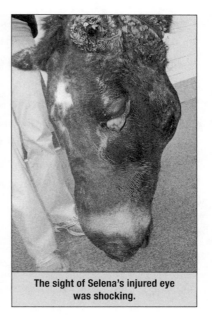

The sight of Selena's injured eye was shocking.

The theory that her horse ran through a fence doesn't hold up with Proto because Selena's front legs and chest aren't torn up; no pressure lines are evident on her skin. As Proto looks around the pasture, she doesn't see any ripped bushes near the fences, or any new fence posts being put in or old ones being straightened. Later, she drives around the entire farm twice: same thing. Proto believes what really happened that night in the pasture was that Selena got attacked by another horse, a bully Proto says she had previously seen picking on other horses, chasing them across the property, teeth bared. After playing so much polo, she cannot imagine Selena running around the pasture and putting herself through a fence; her normal routine after a match is to eat and immediately go to sleep. Proto believes Selena was so exhausted from her third chukker — the one she made her play — that the twenty-one-year-old mare got chased around the pasture by the dominant horse, run through bushes and other foliage, dropped from exhaustion, and was kicked in the head. Proto can't forgive herself.

Dr. Nick Smith, one of Rood & Riddle's field vets, follows behind the trailer taking Selena to the hospital. He is scared the mare won't make it. He was the first vet called to the farm, and the sight of the mare was one of the most gruesome scenes he has encountered since he graduated from vet school in 2007.

Selena is whisked to a stall outside radiology the moment she arrives at Rood & Riddle. Dr. Brett Woodie performs an emergency tracheotomy so she can breathe. While nursing techs and vets work to stabilize Selena, clean the mud and dirt off her body, and radiograph her head and lacerated limbs, Dr. Claire Latimer, the clinic's specialist in veterinary ophthalmology, talks with Proto outside the emergency stall. Latimer explains that it's not actually the eyeball hanging out of Selena's eye, but her third eyelid, or what's called the nictitating membrane. It is normally tucked behind the lid in the inner corner of the eye, but on Selena it is so swollen it can't fit. The third eyelid acts as a windshield wiper: Horses can pull their globes back in and flash the membrane across the surface of the cornea to protect it, or remove something such as dust. Latimer has seen her share of exploded eyeballs, but often when she has a horse with a third eyelid as swollen as Selena's, the globe behind it is intact. They will have to wait until the swelling goes down to know for sure. However, even if it is intact, Latimer doesn't know if the third eyelid will survive; for now, the vet will have to keep the exposed tissue from drying out until it can fit back in its inside pocket.

Selena's radiographs show that despite the lacerations and swelling, the horse doesn't have any damage to her skull or left hind cannon bone. She needs surgery to repair the wounds on her legs and clean out dirt that could cause infection, but she won't be anesthetized until she's stable. Her immediate treatment includes fluids, antibiotics, and analgesics given intravenously, as well as anti-inflammatory drugs. The bulging eyelid is packed with gel and

Selena's head wrapped with gauze and bandages. She is moved to the intensive care unit.

***

One of the biggest problems for veterinarians is that their patients can't talk. No one will ever know what truly happened to Selena. But Woodie doesn't need Selena to talk to see how much pain she is in over the next forty-eight hours. Despite the fentanyl patches and pain medications, he can tell it hurts her even to move. She appears terribly depressed, her head constantly down. Yet it turns out that Selena knows how to take care of herself.

Horses have two kinds of sleep: slow-wave, while standing, and paradoxical, a deeper REM sleep where they must lie down. (They also have a drowsy standing state.) Horses guard each other while they sleep, both in the wild and in paddocks; they are creatures of flight, genetically wired to escape predators. But an injured horse needs more rest and more sleep than normal. Despite being alone in a strange place that must be frightening, Selena immediately lies down and gives herself the rest and sleep she needs to heal. But she doesn't overdo it, which would make her vulnerable to secondary problems (such as sores and pneumonia).

In only two days, the swelling in her left hind leg is down enough for Woodie to clean and debride the wounds (remove dead tissue) and put a drain in the largest one to evacuate fluid. After three days of treatment, the swelling is down in Selena's eye and Latimer can see the globe is intact. But the horse can't blink correctly; it's unclear at this stage whether the problem is a mechanical or neurological problem, but without being able to spread her tear film, she won't be able to take care of her cornea. Also, Latimer sees Selena has hemorrhaged into the cornea itself, which is unusual; it doesn't endanger her eyesight but it does signify the strength of the blow to her head.

But despite her age, Selena is trim and strong and healthy, an athlete, not an out-of-shape paddock potato, a tubby binge eater. This makes all the difference, as it would with a human. Over the coming weeks the healing of her multiple wounds, including her eye, progresses steadily. She stays at Rood & Riddle until mid-February. When she is released, her vision appears normal. But during her rehabilitation, after it is apparent the pain is increasing in her left hind limb, she is diagnosed with laminitis and has to return to the clinic. Laminitis, as previously mentioned in Chapter 3 on Victor's Pursuit, is a complex, baffling, and sometimes deadly disease. It occurs when the laminae, the tissue that hold the hoof wall to the coffin bone (the bottommost bone in the leg), become inflamed and break down. With Selena, the edema (swelling) in her left hind leg has resulted in significant inflammation and restricted blood flow to her left hind foot. The situation is serious. However, her laminitis is in a hind leg not a front, which carries more of the horse's weight, and X-rays show her coffin bone, while rotating, is not sinking. Dr. Robert Agne treats Selena aggressively with specialized shoes, anti-inflammatories, and various other medications and treatments. Her supporting hind limb stays healthy. The laminitis begins to mend, and after two weeks she leaves Rood & Riddle again for a hospital barn at Caddel Equine Therapy Center in nearby Georgetown for further recovery. The bills are getting higher.

People assume Mia Proto is wealthy because her dad is a politician and a banker, because she plays polo and went to private school. Her family has a Thoroughbred breeding farm (albeit a small one) and the home in which she grew up is historic. Her great-grandmother was even an Italian baroness on the island of Capri.

But now at nineteen, Proto tells me she is expected by her family to pay her own way as much as possible. Her dad takes care of her tuition, but she pays the rest — room, board, and expenses — by

Selena, with owner Mia Proto, recuperated well.

working two jobs. Because her family is helping her with Selena's bills (around $32,000, more than $16,000 at Rood & Riddle alone), that means she is now also expected to graduate in three years instead of four from the University of Kentucky's new equine science and management program. However, a horse owner is often no different from a mother: If sacrifices need to be made, Proto will make them. She moves to an apartment in a bad neighborhood, lives on Ramen noodles, forgoes new clothes and sneakers and thoughts of spring breaks in the sun. The college student is more mature than many, which makes it easier. She has her life planned out: She wants to own and run a Thoroughbred broodmare farm similar to the larger, neighboring one she worked on growing up where stakes-winner Sharp Humor, a son of noted sire Distorted Humor, was foaled. Her boyfriend is seven years older and owns a dairy farm back home; she's known him since she was fourteen. They'll settle on his property after college. She's so serious and well-spoken — no "ums" or "likes" or statements sounding as if they end in questions — that I'm relieved when the following information is revealed because it reassures me that she hasn't been body-snatched by a thirty-five-year-old: She has the Pussycat Dolls on her iPod; she remains a big fan of Walter Farley's classic children's book, *The Black Stallion*; and she grew up watching AMC's 8 a.m. morning Westerns while eating her cereal, resulting in a passion for John Wayne.

***

Now picture the father: It is May and Frank Proto drives down from New York to take his daughter home from college for the summer and to see Selena at the hospital barn. The horse continues to recover but she'll likely never play polo again. She'll be shipped back up to New York when she's ready. Frank Proto once dreamed of being a horse doc, as he puts it. (His daughter tells me one of the reasons he's not is because he couldn't stand to put horses down.) Now he's a county legislator and bank vice president. He has thick gray hair and green eyes, wears a corduroy jacket, and smokes a pipe. He has an ease about him; he's probably a great party guest. He played polo in college at Cornell under "Doc" Roberts, the well-known veterinary professor and notoriously tough polo coach who died in 2005 at eighty-nine. Roberts once pinned an overly aggressive player against the boards in a Madison Square Garden match not soon forgotten by anyone who was there.

I ask Frank what kind of person plays polo, the game Argentine player Gonzalo Pieres once said "should be played with hot blood and a cool head."

"To play polo," Frank says, "you have to be a little nuts. Who in their right mind would get on a pony going forty-five miles an hour waving a stick?" We're in his silver truck, his daughter is driving, he's shotgun, I'm in the back. We're en route to see Selena. The power steering went out on Frank's drive down from New York, and he keeps telling his daughter to slow down on the narrow country roads. "And we didn't even have the helmets you guys have now," he says. "We had these leather helmets that looked like something out of an old Ronald Reagan war movie."

A great polo horse, Frank says, is gutsy. "Size is important but not key; they shouldn't be more than 16 hands and should be smart, quick learners. They have to want to play. Winning depends as much on the horse as it does on you."

As we drive on, Frank tells me his daughter got her first polo lesson at age twelve, when she weighed forty pounds soaking wet. They got her up on Speedy, now passed away, who in his prime was one of Cornell's top polo ponies. Selena was bought the following year and Mia started to play seriously. In talking about the sport once, Mia told me, "It's a rush. In a car, if you're going forty to forty-five miles an hour … it doesn't seem very fast, but when you're on the back of a horse, you're flying. The ground is a blur. When I play, I don't hear the crowd. I can only hear the horses and the people I'm playing with. It's like being in your own world, flying around completely unprotected, about an inch from death."

We arrive at the hospital barn. In the stall Selena looks healthy and serene — just a little cloudy spot in her eye, her leg looks like it's healing, you can barely see the tracheotomy wound. Mia brushes the dust from her coat while her father fusses over this nice old lady, as he calls her. He's relieved to see Selena fat — she's gained forty-two pounds. Mia's relieved that her personality hasn't changed; she's still somewhat dignified and reticent. The co-owner of the hospital barn, Linda Caddel, says Selena was one of the worst trauma cases she has ever seen.

Almost everyone knows someone who has experienced a near miss — like a kid in a car accident whose spinal cord was an inch from being severed. In Selena's case, a little more eye damage, and she could have lost the eye. She was close to severe skull fractures. She could have had nerve damage in and around the upper part of her airway, causing paralysis. The laceration on her left hind leg could have reached the joint, setting her up for an infection, and the laminitis had the potential to be fatal. "She walked the edge," says Woodie, "and luckily she was on the right side."

Back in the truck, as father and daughter head out, they tell me that ever since she started playing polo, Mia has been routinely thrown at walls without serious injury. OK, she's sprained her ankle, broken some fingers, and her right arm is scarred from where she was tossed into the chicken wire above the boards at one match. But her luck has held, too. We talk on and Frank recalls how they got her excused from gym growing up — Mia had to prove she had six hours of physical activity a week, and that came from only one polo practice. We turn off onto the freeway. "She's the best polo player in the family," Frank says, and then admonishes his daughter again to slow down.

Selena remains retired and healthy in Slaterville Springs, New York.

Lucky

The trailer pulled up to Barn 9 after a two-and-a-half-hour drive from Louisa, a town in eastern Kentucky. The referring vet had called ahead: A foal, a family pet roughly six weeks old, had been mauled by a stallion. It was touch and go. His owners were desperate to save him. Dr. Alexandra Tracey, an intern at Rood & Riddle, was waiting at the barn for the trailer. She assumed the colt would be on the floor when they opened the door.

The door opened and a snack-size chestnut Tennessee Walker was standing without a problem, docilely nursing from his mother, Rose. It was Lucky … again.

The foal, originally christened Red, had been at Rood & Riddle three and a half weeks earlier. At that time, he'd had Salmonella, and the infection had gone into his hip. He was lame in his right front foot, and X-rays showed he had an infection in the coffin bone. At that age, with those medical problems, he easily could have died. He went home after a week on the mend. But trouble preceded the Salmonella: When the foal was a week and a half old, he had gotten his head firmly wedged under a fence, but had the sense to lie there without moving until morning when Gene Wilson, the husband and father of the family that owned him, could extricate him. His life was actually problematic from birth: Rose initially wouldn't let him nurse. Her first foal had died; no one saw what happened, but it was thought she had stepped on it, accidentally or intentionally. When Rose finally allowed Lucky to nurse, it had to be supervised to make sure he wasn't harmed. Now, the inquisitive colt, whose father had died after getting tangled up in barbed wire a month before he was born, was back at Rood & Riddle. The stallion on the Wilsons' farm, Willie, had a habit of figuring out how to open doors. He had broken the latch to the door of the barn where the colt and his mother were stabled, and then nudged the door open slightly with his head. The foal darted through the cracked door to the open pasture to say hello to the stallion. Not a good idea.

Willie is small and black and known to be nasty. Although many stallions are bad-tempered and aggressive, especially toward other stallions, Pauletta Wilson, Gene's wife, believes Willie has insecurities about his size. In addition, he had never liked the foal's father, who had often put the smaller stallion in his place. When the foal trotted into Willie's pasture, a neighbor driving by saw the black stallion go after him as if he meant to kill him. Willie split the foal's head with his hoof and bit him multiple times on the neck, trapping the colt between his two front feet. It looked as if Willie was trying to stomp the foal into the ground. Blood stained the grass. Then Willie left him for dead within ten feet of where the foal's father is buried and went off grazing at the far end of the pasture. Meanwhile, the neighbor had found Gene on the property and told him what happened.

From a distance, Gene and Pauletta thought the foal was dead. By the time they got to him, the colt was still lying where Willie had left him, moaning. The foal's head was a mess. Gene pulled him to the barn on a canvas tarp and called his vet. He told her he'd pay her fine if she got a speeding ticket getting there. When Dr. Liza McVicker ar-

Lucky's horrific wounds made his case tenuous.

rived from Equine Medical Center in Chesapeake, Ohio, about forty-five minutes away, the colt was a sight. The vet could see his frontal bone through the open wound in his head. Yet she was surprised to find it wasn't fractured. But McVicker was worried about internal injuries and knew the foal had to get to a hospital quickly. She sewed the foal's head up, started him on pain meds, and inserted a catheter in his neck to administer fluids to stabilize him. She worked as fast as she could, her adrenalin flowing. The Wilsons and their adult daughter, Lara, watched McVicker and her assistant work, as did a family friend, Larry West, who had been helping Gene clear brush when the attack happened. Larry looked at the prone foal. "If the little guy makes it," he told them, "you need to call him Lucky."

Ten miles down the road on the drive to Lexington, the foal got to his feet and tried to get under the partition separating him from his mother in order to nurse. Gene stopped the truck so they could move the foal over next to Rose. The colt stood the rest of the way.

When the trailer arrived at Rood & Riddle and Tracey saw Lucky was alive, she assumed he'd need an immediate blood transfusion. But surprisingly, his blood counts, plus clinical signs such as him walking off the trailer without a problem, demonstrated Lucky didn't need it. She replaced his catheter and started him on various medications. Considering what he'd been through, Lucky didn't look bad from the outside, even with a stitched-up head. The vets thought, however, he likely had a concussion. He also had abrasions and contusions (bruises) on his neck, chest, thorax, and abdomen. When Tracey felt the open wound (about two inches in diameter) on the foal's neck where it met the chest over his left pectoral muscle, she could feel severe damage.

Dr. Stephen Reed, the lead vet on the case, thought it was a miracle the stallion hadn't torn a hole in the foal's esophagus. If the stallion had hit the jugular or the carotid artery, Lucky could have died. But Lucky had cheated death again. Still, the damage was great, and the foal was in shock. His prognosis was guarded.

***

A week later, Tracey and Andrea Whittle, one of Rood & Riddle's night supervisors, were giving Lucky a back scratch. He was standing still, enjoying it. But the left side of his neck was a shocking sight. Roughly three quarters of the skin was now gone. The area of exposed, ruptured muscle looked like blood-soaked raw meat. For anyone not used to medical sights, it was horrifying, a stomach-turner. Here's what had happened: In the past week, bacteria, gaining access through the open wound on Lucky's neck, caused abscesses to form on both sides of his neck between the skin and the muscle. The warm, moist environment was a breeding ground for infection. Dr. Brett Woodie performed surgery to open the abscesses and put a drain on each side of Lucky's neck to create exit routes for fluid. Additional skin and muscle then died, causing the wound on the left side to enlarge. In a second surgery the left side was debrided (dead tissue removed), and more dead skin peeled off the already-gaping area ... all of this resulting in a wince-inducing sight. Tracey had never seen a wound that severe. Whittle had only once before, when two foals had accidentally gotten switched at a barn, and one of the mares kicked the unfamiliar baby that had been put back with her.

When the Wilsons' daughter told Reed she wanted to drive from Louisa to see Lucky, Reed told her, "It's really bad. It's not what you expect." When Lara arrived, approached the stall, and saw the exposed wound, she did a double take. She kept asking Reed: "Is he going to make it? Is the skin going to grow back? Is he going to look like a regular horse?" He assured her all that was possible. Lara thought the vet was crazy, but didn't say it out loud. She took pictures with her camera phone and repeated Reed's assurances to her incredulous parents when they saw the shots.

Despite everything that had happened, Lucky was a happy foal. Tennessee Walkers are known for their easygoing nature, their calm and hardiness. Back in the stall with Tracey, Lucky leaned into her backrub. "Oh, you Frankenbaby," she said, keeping clear of the wound. "It's a good thing you're cute."

Reed stopped by the stall and examined the foal. "I'd like to get him in a place where we can hose him down (to clean him up)," he said to Tracey and Whittle. He reminded them to spray the wound with scarlet oil twice a day. The anti-bacterial would speed the healing. In a coincidence, McVicker had been one of Reed's students at

Ohio State, where Reed had taught for over twenty-five years before coming to Rood & Riddle in 2007, the year McVicker graduated. The young vet had been one of Reed's few students whose handwriting was clear enough to read. He was pleased to see her job on stitching up the foal's head had been just as neat.

After looking at Lucky for a while, you got used to the grotesqueness of his wound. Rood & Riddle surgeons couldn't close it because there wasn't enough skin. What was there would be like suturing tissue paper. If all went well, granulation tissue would form a bed of tissue that would fill the wound level with the surrounding skin. The wound's edges would contract to cover the granulation tissue with skin.

However, with an open wound like his, an infection could easily start and become deep-seated in the muscle. It was summer, flies were in the air, and the wound was itchy. Lucky had to be watched constantly to keep him from rubbing the area too hard against the side of the stall, the feed bucket, and the water pail, creating more tissue trauma. If his blood supply didn't stay strong, the edges of the wounds on both sides of his neck could die off further, making the open wounds expand instead of contract. Woodie was worried about the jugular vein and associated nerves that were exposed. If any of those were damaged, the foal could have a loss of nerve function to the left side of his larynx. In addition, it was important to keep the foal's pain under control so he'd keep eating and stay healthy.

Tracey knew if the foal took a downward turn, it would be hard to turn him back around. While she was rubbing Lucky down in the stall, another foal came into Rood & Riddle that had apparently been kicked in the head by another horse. Despite surgery, that foal died three days later after lapsing into a coma. In a couple of months, yet another foal would come in that had been attacked by dogs, family pets, no less. He would die as well.

Intern Dr. Sarah Gray visits Lucky at Sarah Weed's lay-up barn.

Tracey needed to check on some other cases. As she left Lucky's stall, the foal nipped her playfully. "You're a devil in a foal suit," she told him.

***

It was July, humid and hot, when Lucky came to the hospital. Across the city, even the grass was getting sunburned. The heat didn't help in the colt's second week at Rood & Riddle, where one of the biggest challenges was keeping his fever down. It was running around 103; the anti-inflammatories would keep it down to a safer 101, but when they started to wear off, it would rise again. (The normal temperatures for foals range from 100.5 to 101.5.) The meds could be given only twice a day due to potentially harmful side effects such as kidney problems. Lucky's IV fluids were refrigerated until they were given, which helped reduce his core temperature. However, his red blood cell count had to be watched; an excess of fluids would make it drop; they needed to be strictly regulated. The foal got alcohol baths regularly, and two fans remained on all the time in the stall. However, it was difficult to keep the fans positioned correctly twenty-four hours a day; when Lucky was down sleeping, the air wasn't hitting him. When his fever went to the high end, he lost interest in nursing and lay down to sleep. Yet vets didn't want to kill the fever entirely because it was part of his immune system working to fight infection. It was a balancing act. By the end of the second week he had stabilized. The wounds on his neck were also mending. Lucky was ready to be transferred to a hospital barn, Three Sisters Farm.

The drama of the stallion attack and the scrappiness of Lucky's personality made him one of the in-house celebrities at Rood & Riddle that summer. The day Lucky left to go to Three Sisters, staff members were sorry to see him leave. It was hard to gripe or be crabby once you had been around him. The foal saw the glass half-full.

Three Sisters — owned by Sarah Weed, then a Rood & Riddle employee — is located about twenty minutes from the hospital on fifty quiet acres with a wooded view near the town of Midway. Lara Wilson and her father came to see Lucky there the day he was transferred.

At the farm, the barn is black with white trim, with varnished wood on the inside. Each stall has a wine-colored door and a window. Lara and Gene approached the stall where Rose and Lucky stood. Lucky had his nose down in a bucket licking a salt block. Gene hadn't seen the foal since the day of the attack. He blanched when he saw the smaller open wound on the right side of the foal's neck where a drain remained.

"Dad," said Lara, "that's his good side."

Despite Gene's shock after he saw the left side, he was relieved to see the foal up and about. He and his family hadn't owned Lucky's father, a show horse, all his life, but as far as they knew, no other offspring existed. The Wilsons had been hoping Rose would birth a colt to carry on the bloodline, even though they don't compete anymore. Lucky's grandfather is a renowned show horse and stallion: Gen's Armed and Dangerous. In pictures of him, with his proud stance, gleaming sorrel coat, and flaxen mane, he looks like the World Grand Champion he is, and resembles Trigger Jr., one of the Tennessee Walkers Roy Rogers rode on his show after replacing the first Trigger, a Palomino.

Tennessee Walkers have been in Gene Wilson's family since 1947. When his great-uncle died in the 1960s, his widow told Gene to come pick out one of her late husband's horses. Gene was in law school at the University of Kentucky at the time and took Snoop, as the horse was called, back to school. Snoop also came from esteemed bloodlines — World Grand Champions Merry Go Boy and Midnight Sun were in his pedigree. Gene boarded Snoop at The Red Mile racetrack in Lexington, in the barn of the late equine artist Allen Brewer Jr. (who was said to keep horse fetuses in glass jars in his studio to study their anatomy). The Red Mile has been a harness racing track since 1875. When Gene would ride Snoop out on the racetrack for exercise, people in the other barns complained, saying their horses were jealous because Snoop didn't have to pull a sulky.

Gene got Snoop when the horse was four years old; Snoop lived until he was thirty. Many people outside the equine world don't realize how long horses live, how their owners can pass from one life stage to another, with a horse as a constant family member and friend. In Snoop's prime, "there wasn't a horse in Larch County who could keep up with him," according to Gene. It was Willie,

Lucky enjoyed some turnout with his dam, Rose, at a lay-up farm.

Snoop's grandson, who tried to kill Lucky. In the chaos right after the attack, as McVicker and her assistant attended to Lucky, Gene paced around the mauled foal and said he was going to go put Willie down, right then and there. McVicker and her assistant convinced him not to do it when he was so upset. Think about it, they said, don't do anything you'll regret. You can always come back and do it later.

***

"The horse I'm going to see at Sarah Weed's is a little foal that got savaged by a stallion," said Reed, on the phone to Dr. Scott Morrison, the hospital's head of podiatry. Another week had passed, making it three since the mauling. Reed was talking on his cell as he drove out to Three Sisters to see Lucky. Dr. Sarah Gray, an intern, and I, were accompanying him. "Yeah. Well, in any event, this foal is over at the knees now. And I assume it's just because he's been penned up all of his life. The question is: Do I just tell her to start giving him more exercise now? Or do I need for you to come look at him to get some corrective trimming? Do you put extensions on his toes? Raise his toes? What's the right thing? …"

We were on a narrow country road. Because of their breakneck schedules, most of the hospital's veterinarians conduct business from their cars. Some are on the high end of the distractibility scale, including Reed. The vet sometimes reminded me of Lieutenant Columbo from the old detective TV series; both were as brilliant as they were absentminded. The car drifted toward the center of the road and oncoming traffic. Gray and I looked at each other wide-eyed. Reed veered back to the right side of the road as he listened to Morrison. Exhale.

"… All right … He's not knuckling over but he's kind of far forward. It's just so worrisome. I mean this poor man, the foal's been in the clinic — they had a Salmonella osteomyelitis. We got it through that. Then it got *this* problem. This thing has had more than $1,000 a week in vet bills since birth. And now, he's healing from all that, and he's over at the knees! (Listens) … So stack the bandages on twelve hours, off twelve hours, more exercise, and then after that, if that doesn't work you may have to put some toe extensions on. All right … I'll try and take a picture today and bring it back for you. All right. That's what I'll do. Thanks, Scott. Bye."

The danger with Lucky being over at the knees was that his tendons could permanently contract. If that happened, his front legs would be crooked and he could have difficulty getting around. When we reached the farm, Reed relayed Morrison's instructions to Weed. "Stacking" the bandages, or wrapping the entire limb from fetlock to elbow, would relax the contracted tendons and ligaments. Then Gray took the staples out of the foal's forehead, as Reed simultaneously supervised and asked Weed about the details of her upcoming wedding. One of the hospital's techs once told me he thought Reed should have been an anthropologist; he was so infinitely interested in everyone and everything, including, on this day, the fact that Weed did not have the shoes to go with her dress yet. The tech noted the Columbo factor as well: "And he seems so scattered. But then he'll come back to you ten minutes later and ask you about whatever you're talking about. He doesn't miss a thing." When Gray was done, Reed gently pointed out that a bit of staple, about half the length of an eyelash, had fallen to the barn floor. "A good vet doesn't leave anything on the floor," he said.

Save for the knees, the foal was making great progress. But a week later, he didn't look right. His energy was low, and he was depressed and lethargic. Both the conjunctiva (the pink membrane) rimming his eyes and his (oral) mucous membranes were pale. It turned out he was anemic. An ultrasound of his lungs also showed the beginnings of pneumonia. Reed was worried the foal would seriously deteriorate. The vet put him on antibiotics and high-protein feed to boost his energy level and build muscle mass. Lucky's anemia was being caused in large part by inflammation from the pneumonia. Resolving the pneumonia would also eventually take care of the anemia.

As far as his knees, after three days of the bandages, they still weren't better. Morrison came out to assess the situation and trim the foal's hooves. The vet thought once the foal could be turned out, the problem would clear up. The growth process of the long bones in his limbs had stalled because of his long confinement. Morrison believed once Lucky got exercise, the ligaments and tendons would stretch, and the knees would straighten out. As Lucky progressed that's what happened. Eventually, Weed was able to leave him and the mare out all day. Being outside was the best medicine. His anemia and pneumonia receded and then disappeared. On the quiet farm, summer turned to fall, and the cicadas' drone grew fainter. Lucky played and grew and returned to health.

***

Lucky came back to Rood & Riddle the last Sunday in September. He'd have his final check-up on Monday and leave for his real home the following day. The wound on his neck had contracted to an opening about one to two inches wide and four inches long; it looked like just a small laceration. He had no nerve damage to his neck, and plenty of muscle remained for him to have normal movement. He might never have a normal contour to his neck, and it would probably always feel bumpy to touch. But he was alive. He was bigger, his

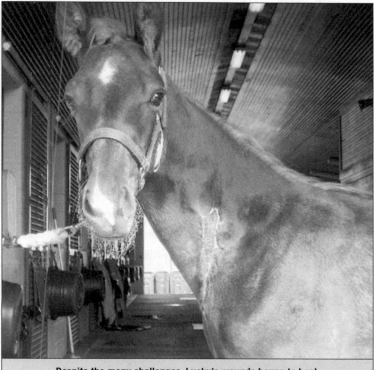

Despite the many challenges, Lucky's wounds began to heal.

coat darker, his face more mature. His mane had turned flaxen, his coat sorrel. He looked much like his grandfather. He wasn't a baby anymore.

That Sunday, as he and Rose waited in the stall to go home, and the Wilsons made arrangements in Louisa to pick him up, another sort of homecoming was taking place in Louisville: the memorial service for Eight Belles at Churchill Downs. The racetrack's bugler played "Call to the Post" to open the service, and the speakers came to the podium in the garden where the filly's remains were interred in a handmade walnut box. A magnolia tree sent from a South Carolina fan shaded her grave. After two people spoke, Larry Jones, Eight Belles' trainer, took the podium. He wore his trademark white Stetson and a sport jacket. He spoke of watching a "long-legged, gangly two-year-old filly that took a while to learn her lessons ... " turn into a "lovely, gallant, and courageous racehorse."

Of Eight Belles' breakdown, Jones said, "It was something we never, ever dreamed, and we'll never understand." He spoke of trying to find some peace about it, and how he was "arguing with the One that's in charge of all, and I couldn't understand why He took *my* filly, and Mr. (Rick) Porter's filly, and had this end this way.

"But it was revealed to me, thank goodness," Jones said, "this was not our filly, this was His filly a long time before we knew her, and He had a plan for her, and we don't understand it all, but we are seeing it unfold today. We're going to see it unfold in the future ... Changes are going to be made because of her ... She proved through all the conflict and all the accusations that she competed at the very greatest horse race in the world without the help of performance-enhancing drugs. And therefore, if she didn't need it, no racehorse needs it." The day before, the governor of Kentucky banned the use of anabolic steroids for Thoroughbred and Standardbred racehorses.

" … She stole a piece of my heart," Jones said. His voice broke. He stopped for a moment, put his hand to his mouth, and started to cry. "When she fell that day, she ripped a big part of my heart right out with her." He told Eight Belles to rest in peace and left the microphone. Two and a half weeks later, Jones announced he planned to retire from training at the end of 2009. He said the tragedy of Eight Belles combined with overly demanding racehorse owners had taken too much out of him.

The day after the memorial service, Reed and Woodie gave Lucky the okay to go home. In the end, Gene didn't have the heart to put down Willie. Instead, he spent $8,000 on new fencing to keep the black stallion safely contained. Lucky's combined medical bills approached $30,000. When the Wilsons picked him up, it was one of the first brisk days of fall. It was also the second day of the September yearling sale at Keeneland in Lexington, when some of the most desirable Thoroughbred youngsters in the world are sold. Right as the Wilsons and Lucky hit the road for home, a filly at Keeneland was sold for $800,000, followed by a colt for $285,000. On the sale's first day, a filly sired by the great A.P. Indy was purchased for $3.1 million by Sheikh Mohammed bin Rashid al Maktoum, the ruler of Dubai. Although Lucky is a pet, he had received medical care fit for any of those Thoroughbreds, and he is surely loved as much as Jones loved his dark gray filly. Lucky wasn't only lucky; he was blessed.

About six months after Lucky left the hospital he started showing signs of neurological difficulties and returned to Rood & Riddle where he had surgery for wobbler's syndrome (compression of the spinal cord). Dr. Stephen Reed believes the stallion may have damaged the vertebrae in Lucky's neck during the attack. The hope was that the surgery, combined with the fact that Lucky was still growing and his bones remodeling (repairing and strengthening), would eventually result in him being able to live comfortably. As this book went to press, Lucky was still mending. "He's a tough horse," said Reed after Lucky left the hospital for the third time in less than a year. "He does not want to die. He just keeps trying to live." For the most recent update on the colt, check http://www.equineer.blogspot.com.

CHAPTER

11

Sid

Sherri Wilson bred her Clydesdale mare to a champion New York Clyde using artificial insemination several years ago, but the birth was problematic, and the foal died thirty-six hours later. In 2006, Wilson said what the hell, and bred the mare to one of her Friesian stallions. In July 2007 Sid was born. He came out brown like a Clyde, but more refined: a smaller head, finer bones. He had one white stocking on his left hind leg. He'd never be graded by the Dutch breeding associations like some of her other Friesians because he wasn't purebred, but he became Wilson's frisky prince, her favorite lawn ornament. He was reminiscent of Scooby-Doo in his clumsiness. Sid, by his owner's admission, was spoiled: He used to lie in her lap as a foal and wander around loose in her indoor arena as he grew. He liked to come up on the deck and wait for her outside the house like a dog.

Wilson and her husband, Don, loved to watch the little guy kicking it up, running around. But when the colt got to be around six months old, Don kept saying, "I don't know if he looks right."

Because the colt has the Clydesdale feathering covering his

hooves, by the time they figured out a couple of months later that he was running on the tops of his toes like a ballet dancer en pointe, it was almost too late.

Wilson had read about Rood & Riddle in one of her horse magazines. From various articles, she knew Dr. Scott Morrison, the hospital's head of podiatry, is one of the top people in the country when it comes to equine feet.

Sid had one of the worst cases of clubfoot syndrome that Morrison had ever seen, but he tried not to show his surprise as he examined the colt in front of Wilson during the initial evaluation. The colt was also the first clubfoot case involving both front legs (bilateral) the vet had seen at the hospital. Grading on a scale of 1 through 4, Sid's condition was at grade 4+, the most severe. With grade 4+, the anterior, or forward part, of the hoof wall is at a 90-degree angle or more. Without treatment, Sid's hooves eventually would start to turn over. Once they went beyond vertical, the growth process would lose a counterforce and problems would snowball. In six months he wouldn't be able to walk, and he'd likely develop laminitis, and sores and holes in his pastern.

The condition, also called ballerina syndrome, happens when the tendons of a horse's legs are contracted and don't stretch as fast as the long bones grow. It can be congenital or developmental, and ranges in type and severity. In humans, clubfoot is congenital; there are some similarities to the equine version but many differences. Although Assault, the 1946 Triple Crown winner, was dubbed "The Club-Footed Comet," he actually got the odd shape of his right front hoof (and subsequent limp at a walk or trot, but not a gallop) from stepping on what was believed to be a surveyor's stake as a foal. His foot became infected, and part of the hoof had to be cut away and replaced with a special shoe. He didn't have true clubfoot syndrome like Sid, and it's rare for any Thoroughbred

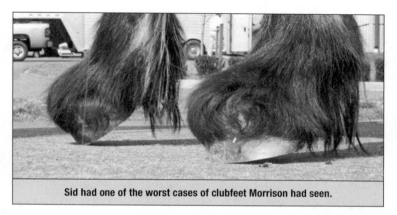

Sid had one of the worst cases of clubfeet Morrison had seen.

with a severe case to become an athlete because the stress is too much for its legs and feet. (However, some humans born with club-foot have been known not only to overcome it, but also to become unforgettable athletes, people like Olympic soccer star Mia Hamm and former Dallas Cowboys quarterback Troy Aikman.)

During the evaluation Morrison inspected each of the colt's coronary bands, the circles of vascular tissue located at the top of the hoof wall. A hoof's growth springs from there, and the vet was checking to see if the colt had laminitis, which he did not. Morrison shot radiographs to look at the health of the coffin bone and the degree of misalignment in the joint. The coffin bone, or third phalanx, is the primary bone in a horse's foot. Located inside the hoof capsule (like a body in a coffin), it bears much of a horse's weight.

Sid's coffin bone was healthy. He didn't have bone disease from it being loaded abnormally for a long time. Yet he would need a coffin bone realignment, with shoeing and trimming by Morrison. Then surgeon Brett Woodie would perform a tenotomy, in which Sid's tendons would be cut to release them. Doing so would create a gap that would eventually fill in with scar tissue, creating artificial length and allowing the heels to lower and position properly. (In less severe cases of clubfoot syndrome, special shoeing alone over time will straighten out the problem.) With Sid being young and healthy, the prognosis was good for him to be pasture sound, barring any complications. He'd never be a high-level performance horse, but that wasn't his path anyway.

Normally, Morrison could numb a colt and do his part with the animal standing. But Sid wasn't accustomed to standing for anyone so he was put under anesthesia.

One of the first people in history to recognize that equine medicine is as multi-layered and complicated as human medicine was an unsuccessful military man turned scholar, Marcus Terentius Varro, who lived during the Roman Empire (according to the 1996 book *Veterinary Medicine* by Robert H. Dunlop and David J. Williams). Varro split veterinary care into two categories: one for all the problems a smart shepherd could handle; the other for problems requiring an astute surgeon. Varro was a forward-thinking man — prescient, for example, in recognizing the phenomenon of contagion in animals — but I wonder if he could have imagined this modern-day operating room where Sid lay for his procedure. The colt was hooked up to a machine delivering anesthesia via a tube down his airway, one catheter in his jugular vein delivering intravenous fluids to maintain his blood flow, another inserted into one of the arteries in his face to monitor blood pressure. An electrocardiogram monitored his heart rhythm.

Sid's new feet after two procedures

With Sid on an operating table, Morrison started taking the colt's heels down with a regular battery-powered sander and sandpaper; they had grown too much to counteract the toes that were wearing off from the pressure of walking on them. It only took a couple of minutes. Wilson, watching from the observation window, thought, "Oh my God. There's just little stubs left." Then the vet sanded the entire hoof wall. With a rubbery acrylic-like substance, similar to Bondo, plus a material made of carbon fiber and Kevlar (the material used to make bulletproof vests), Morrison built a layer of toe, wrapped it tightly in plastic wrap, let it dry for five minutes, and started over. He often thought the process was like fixing a dent in a car. After about six layers, the new toe was built.

Then, an aluminum egg-bar, or round, shoe with a horizontal heel extension was nailed on for further stability. With the reconstruction, not only would Sid look more normal, he'd land normally on his feet, and the weight would be distributed correctly, keeping the coffin bone aligned. He'd need to come back to make sure everything was progressing correctly while the surgery he was about to have healed.

Nurses moved Sid into another sterile operating room so Woodie could perform the tenotomy. For Woodie, Sid's clubfeet were also some of the most troublesome he had ever seen. The surgeon made an incision on the outside of the colt's left front leg. He dissected down to the deep digital flexor tendon in the mid-cannon region, isolated it, and severed the tendon. Then he did the other leg. The worry in the operation is undercorrection (not enough release) or overcorrection, where the toe would rise off the ground from the heel. Woodie flexed and extended Sid's lower limbs. He'd gotten a four- to five-inch release. He gave Wilson the thumbs-up and closed Sid up. Now everyone would have to wait to see how the colt did over the coming weeks to determine if the operation was a success. Woodie was both worried and optimistic, a normal state for him.

After the procedures, Wilson went back to the Holiday Inn to grab a shower and then ran over to the I-Hop for an omelet. She also called and checked on the horses at home. She and her husband own a convenience store and motel near their farm in Bloomfield, Indiana, but her real job is being a slave to five Friesian stallions, three Friesian mares, a miniature pony, a Halflinger, a deaf and blind old donkey, a Tennessee Walker, and, of course, Sid and his mom. Her husband sometimes gets annoyed with her for not trusting that he's done things just right for her brood, but they had two pregnant mares that spring, and she wasn't leaving anything to chance.

Wilson has been horse-crazy since age five. It is an acute condition that strikes millions of little girls. Theories vary as to why this phenomenon happens, but no one seems to be able to explain it: It appears instinctual. The majority of little girls begging for ponies have to settle for the plastic Breyer horses author Melissa Holbrook Pierson called "horses for people who can't have horses" in her book about the link between women and equines, *Dark Horses and Black Beauties: Animals, Women, a Passion* (W.W. Norton, 2000).

Wilson's parents had the same reaction to her condition that many horsewomen say their parents had: "They thought I was crazy." She bought her first horse at fourteen, saving money from her job as a trail guide in Pennsylvania (pay: $1.50 per ride) to buy a buckskin Quarter Horse mare named Paula for $300. Looking back, Wilson thought every girl, given the opportunity, could take the balance and fearlessness learned from riding horses into meeting life.

Wilson's passion now is for Friesians, a Dutch breed that in the Middle Ages carried knights to war. Mostly coal-black, with thick manes and tails, and feathering on their lower legs, they are elegant, a horse of power and mystery. Zorro rode a Friesian. With her long, dark curly hair, 6-foot height, and big personality, Wilson actually reminded one of the vets at Rood & Riddle of a Friesian. Once, an older Dutch man from whom Wilson bought a Friesian kept looking at her a little too long during their conversation. Finally, he asked her to abide by the same rule he and other Friesian breeders apply to their horses' manes and tails: "Don't ever cut that hair."

***

The morning after the tenotomy Sid was doing well ... except he didn't like the food at the hospital. Wilson ran out and bought him some feed he would eat.

Once home, he had a tough time with his new bulletproof hooves. It was almost like he had to learn to walk all over again. When he picked up his feet, they would come up higher than he expected because he wasn't used to bearing his weight flat on his feet. He was also stiff and in pain. He couldn't walk far. Cutting the tendon had stretched other structures, such as the joint capsule and collateral ligaments, putting them in new positions. All he wanted to do was lie in his stall. Wilson got him up four times a day and walked him from one end of the barn to the other, about 200 feet. It left him exhausted, and she was worried. Then he stopped eating for a week. Veterinarians thought the Bute (pain-reliever and anti-inflammatory medication phenylbutazone) might be upsetting his stomach in paste form, so Wilson crushed up tablets in blackstrap molasses, and he started eating again. She would lie with him in the stall, reading aloud. Wilson is a prolific reader who prefers deft, complicated stories. She read Sid *The Kite Runner* — the novel about an Afghani boy's journey to manhood — among others, as the weeks passed and the chill left the air.

Eventually, Sid started getting better but still put his feet down hard. You could hear him coming a mile away. Seven weeks after the operation, Wilson brought him back to Rood & Riddle to see if he was mending correctly ... and he was. X-rays revealed that the coffin bone was still perfectly balanced and parallel to the ground; the tenotomy site had not recontracted. Morrison used a yellow blowtorch to soften up Sid's soles, grown hard from all the stall

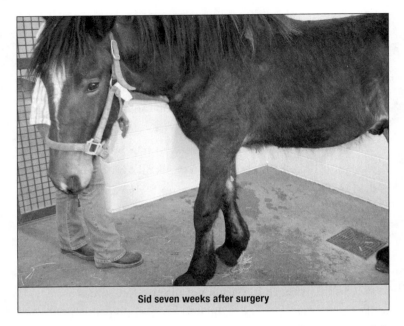

Sid seven weeks after surgery

rest, and then cut the shoe away from the foot with a rasp. He left the artificial toe on as a lever to counteract the continued healing of the tendon. It would probably take six to nine months for Sid's hoof wall to grow in fully at the new angle.

Morrison was pleased with Sid's gait as one of the farriers led the colt in a circle around the examining room. Sid had a goofy elegance, with his Friesian bearing, Clydesdale legs, ten-month-old gangliness. He'd go barefoot for now. As he went back in the stall, Sid accidentally walked into the door. "That's my boy," Wilson said. She loaded him up in her old green trailer with the Friesian sticker on the back.

By fall, there were no more novels for Sid; he preferred running across his favorite terrain on the farm — a three-acre grass lot with a slope and a dip. Sid would run full blast down the expanse and then lie down and roll around for the joy of it, his hooves to the sun.

Steps

Medicine, human or veterinary, is a science that evolves ... like a forest evolves, or a person evolves. Many events play a role in this process: experiments, dreams, accidents, even the whims of nature. For example, blizzards in Colorado in 1949 and 1950 that resulted in numerous range bulls getting frostbitten scrotums led to Colorado State University's veterinary school creating new techniques to gauge bulls' fertility. In 1929, a young German surgical resident, defying his boss' orders, performed the first human heart catheterization — on himself. It was prompted by the resident's fascination with a sixty-five-year-old picture of a horse with a catheter in its heart, an experiment by a French veterinarian and a physiologist. And so, at Rood & Riddle in 2008, the story of a Thoroughbred named Slewpy's Star begins not with Dr. Bonnie Barr in her office day after day trying to think of a way to save the mare dying of pleuropneumonia, but with one of her colleagues, Dr. Michelle LeBlanc, who, as usual, was having trouble falling asleep one night four years earlier.

Two things usually happen when it comes to sleep and LeBlanc, the hospital's insomniac global star in the field of equine reproduction. Either she lies there bug-eyed and is struck with new ideas of how to treat difficult cases, or she falls into a capricious sleep and wakes up struck with new ideas about how to treat them. (One time, she was so excited after having a dream that acupuncture would help a mare with fertility problems, she called the other veterinarian involved early in the morning. She woke him up. After she explained her idea nonstop, there was silence on the other end of the line. Then the veterinarian, a country boy, drawled, "Who do you think you are, Martin Luther King, *having a dream?*")

So this particular night LeBlanc was wrestling in her head with the case of a broodmare with a severely damaged uterine lining and consequent fertility problems. Seen through the endoscope, the scar tissue was so excessive it looked like the tissue of a burn patient. The mare was a new patient for the vet — LeBlanc didn't know what had caused the damage, but it may have been side effects from procaine penicillin infused into the uterus to fight a previous infection. The broodmare might have been particularly sensitive to the medication. She was a valuable horse, and LeBlanc had not come up with a solution. The farm kept saying to her: *Do something*. She had actually sent some pictures of the uterus to an accomplished plastic surgeon whose horses she treated, asking if he had any ideas. His response was, "If this was a burn patient, you'd debride it all and put moist compresses on it." "This is a *uterus*," LeBlanc told him. "I can't do that."

At this same time, a small East Coast biotech start-up, Beech Tree Labs, had developed an experimental drug called detoxified strep-tolysin O, or SLO, to break up scar tissue. The head of the start-up's veterinary side, based in Lexington, had been repeatedly asking LeBlanc to try it. The drug had already been used experimentally for several years with anecdotal success on mares with fertility problems from excessive scar tissue, and Beech Tree wanted hard data.

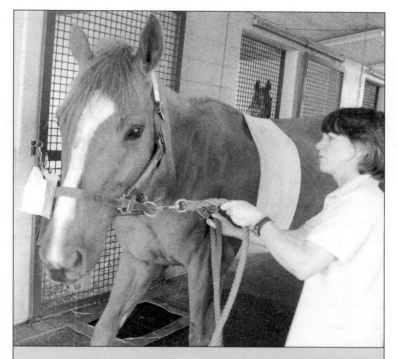

Slewpy's Star in spring 2008 with nursing staff supervisor Alice Campbell; the bandage around her abdomen protects the incision made to drain debris-filled fluid from her chest.

LeBlanc wasn't too enthusiastic because it was so new. But that night, waiting for sleep, the notion came to her to try SLO on the damaged broodmare. "I have no idea if this will work," she said to the farm. "It's free. Let's try it."

Beech Tree describes SLO as "a single molecule, which is a non-toxic form of a bacterial toxin." Detoxifying the molecule revealed an ability to alter scars, says Beech Tree's founder, New York immunologist and virologist Dr. John McMichael. He stumbled across the usage of SLO in treating scar tissue about seven or eight years ago when testing the drug for another purpose — to help with Tourette's-like movement disorders rooted in childhood strep infections. Patients reported not only a reduction in things such as twitches and jerks, but also that their scars had become less visible or had vanished. One woman had badly scarred hands from an accident involving boiling water twenty years earlier. After thirty days on SLO, the scars disappeared. A seventy-year-old male patient with acne scars also saw them go away.

If inflammation continues long enough, the end result is fibrosis, or scar tissue. McMichael says SLO works not only as an anti-inflammatory but it also breaks down old scar tissue and allows it to be replaced by more vital tissue. It also prevents scars in the first place, he says, by stimulating viable cells to fill the gap of the wound. Its use is both for internal and external conditions, from stretch marks to scarring of the heart.

In addition to other projects, Beech Tree Labs is in an initial phase of attempting an FDA study with SLO on workers from the World Trade Center site after the September 11, 2001, attacks. According to McMichael, a significant number of workers who breathed the contaminated air developed idiopathic pulmonary fibrosis, a condition where over time the lungs fill up with scar tissue, resulting in a lack of oxygen being pumped to the brain and other organs. The cause is unknown, no drug exists to remedy it, and many people die within five years after diagnosis from respiratory failure. Anecdotal reports on a handful of patients using SLO for the disease have shown it's helped their respiratory function.

LeBlanc starting giving SLO to the mare with the damaged uterine lining. The mare was bred and got pregnant. LeBlanc stayed cool. "Let's see if she goes all the way," she cautioned. The mare did. Then, "Let's see if the placenta looks OK ... Let's see if the baby looks OK." Everything was fine. The mare got pregnant again two years later. The last LeBlanc heard, she had been sold as a broodmare and was in Asia.

Within a couple of months, LeBlanc got a call from a veterinarian looking for advice on treating a broodmare with adhesions in her vagina after a difficult delivery. The adhesions were surgically removed, but they all came back because of tissue that was still inflamed. She recommended SLO. The veterinarian called back after using it for a while: The adhesions were gone. Soon after, Dr. Scott Morrison, the head of podiatry at Rood & Riddle, was having a major problem with too much scar tissue forming after horses had tenotomies of the deep digital flexor tendon for treatment of laminitis (the tendon is cut in an attempt to stop the rotation of the coffin bone). In some cases, the tissue was so thick, the tendon was recontracting, essentially reversing the surgery. Morrison had resigned himself that there was nothing they could do about it. LeBlanc mentioned SLO. Morrison has also now had success with it numerous times.

Beech Tree has had papers on SLO published in peer-reviewed journals and a study planned for 2009 with an adjunct professor at Yale Medical School. (The focus will be on patients with complications from total knee replacement surgery.) LeBlanc wants to see more hard data on the drug, but she's seen no ill effects. Four years after she first tried it, she got a call from Dr. Bonnie Barr, who works in Rood & Riddle's internal medicine department. Barr was trying to save her patient Slewpy's Star from dying of pleuropneumonia and wanted to know if LeBlanc thought SLO might help. LeBlanc did.

Slewpy's Star is from Oak Haven Farm, a small place in Midway, Kentucky, owned by Linda and Ed Frederick. Four years earlier, the horse had come to Oak Haven from Texas, where the Fredericks have a business partner, as a foal at her dam's side. They raised the foal and sent her back down to Texas for her racing career. The dam's sire was champion Seattle Slew, and she went on to have several more fillies and a colt. A dynasty was born; nearly all the offspring have Slewpy in their names. The colt is nice to be around, but the fillies are not.

"They're mean," Ed Frederick says affectionately of all the female Slewpys, "That's the kind of race filly you want."

The Fredericks both grew up in Lexington and have been in the business for most of their lives.

"It's a gambling life," Linda Frederick said to me one day when I visited them in their cozy office right off Georgetown Road. "You just eat it, breathe it, and live it. You go home, and it doesn't stay in the office."

"The highs are really high," said her husband, "like when you win a $5,000 claiming race. Then you get a stillborn foal and go into a major depression ... (But) we tried to get away from it and couldn't."

One of the biggest lows, say the Fredericks, is losing a horse you care about. In spring 2007, Slewpy's Star's dam died at about sixteen years old. She'd had neurological problems for more than three years, and the Fredericks had spent a "fortune" first trying to help her get well, and then keeping her happy until her time ran out. She was always happiest with a foal by her side, even after she got the point where she couldn't run well alongside it.

Slewpy's Star came back from Texas to Lexington in early February 2008 for her broodmare career. She contracted shipping fever from the trip (a respiratory illness linked to the stress of transport), which then evolved into pleuropneumonia — the worst type of pneumonia. The pleura is a thin cellular membrane that covers the surface of the lungs and lines the thoracic cavity, the interior of the ribs. The thoracic cavity is also called the pleural cavity. With pleuropneumonia, infection and inflammation occur both inside the pleural cavity and the lungs, with fluid building up. The longer pleuropneumonia goes on, the worse it gets, and horses often die from it. The Fredericks could not stand the thought of losing two in a row.

For weeks, the Fredericks tried having a veterinarian treat Slewpy's Star on the farm, but no matter how much pleural fluid was drained, she kept manufacturing more. The fluid started to contain bubbles and scar tissue. Then the scar tissue started to wall off pockets of infection in her chest. The more isolated the infection became, the worse it got. Slewpy's Star wouldn't eat and ended up losing close to 300 pounds. She was sent to Rood & Riddle at the end of March.

Slewpy's Star was at the clinic for a month. She developed thrombosis in her jugular vein (when blockage in the vein occurs due to blood clotting), and IV access wasn't possible; medication such as antibiotics had to be given orally. She had to be monitored to be sure she was drinking enough to stay hydrated. The festering fluid in her chest — full of dead scar tissue, bacteria, pus — was continually drained, and with round-the-clock treatment she improved enough to go home. Yet after a month, she started to worsen and came back.

At Rood & Riddle the second time, Dr. Brett Woodie did a thoracotomy, making an incision in the mare's chest, inserting an endoscope, and flushing out more debris-filled fluid.

Treatment helped considerably, but the infection didn't disappear. Chronic inflammation was producing the scar tissue in her chest: The more scar tissue that was created, the harder it was for her to breathe and the more difficult it was for cells designed to handle invading bacteria to do their job. The mare was also still scary-thin. Her ribs stuck out; her reddish-brown coat was patchy.

Barr kept asking herself what more she could do. Like her beloved Pittsburgh Steelers — the red-haired vet, raised in Pennsylvania, is an unswerving fan — she doesn't mind negotiating tight spots. She thought about how if the horse were a person, they would give her streptokinase, a medication often used after a heart attack to dissolve clots. But it is expensive for human use; for a horse, it would be prohibitive, thousands and thousands of dollars. Barr started asking around the hospital for something to deal with scar tissue and found out about LeBlanc's and Morrison's success using SLO. She and Woodie discussed it and decided that it likely wouldn't hurt, and might help.

Ed Frederick signed a waiver in the event the mare had adverse reactions. He thought it was their last chance. More than twenty years ago he'd had a mare from New York with shipping fever; they were also "pumping gallons of fluid off her lungs." He'd also gambled on what was then an experimental drug for horses: the antibiotic Keflex. He had to drive to the University of Kentucky Medical Center regularly to get it. The mare recovered.

But even though the SLO was free because it was experimental, it still cost, naturally, to keep Slewpy's Star in the hospital. At that time, the Fredericks had two other extremely ill horses at Rood & Riddle. The first was a mare in the intensive care unit with a new foal. After a difficult labor and birth, the mare had developed peritonitis, an infection of the abdominal cavity. Their teaser stallion was at the clinic with Potomac Horse Fever, a dangerous bacterial disease spread by the ingestion of certain aquatic insects and snails. (A teaser's thankless job is to tell if a mare is in heat, setting the stage for the appointment with the stallion.) The bills were mounting. In the horse business, as with farming and love, luck, good or bad, comes in runs. The Fredericks aren't, as Barr put it, "a Jess Jackson or a Dell Hancock," the wealthy owners of two of the biggest Bluegrass horse farms.

In mid-June, Slewpy's Star got her first injection of SLO. Over about the next two weeks, she got SLO every day. Ed Frederick noticed her slow progression toward wellness … she started eating more … then she was moving around more … then she got turned out in the day pen at the front of Rood & Riddle (covered with a blanket so people driving by wouldn't think she was being starved and call authorities).

During her hospital stay Slewpy's Star was, for the most part, quiet, uncharacteristically nice. As she started to recover, she began getting touchy. Then she kicked somebody. "She must be feeling better," said Frederick when Barr told him. At the end of the second week, she was healthy enough to go home.

Barr is cautious about attributing the mare's entire recovery to SLO. She believes it helped as part of the overall treatment but wants to use it in more cases, see more results. Frederick says, "I think it saved her life. I bet she didn't weigh 700 pounds (at 16 hands). She was a skeleton with skin."

At the end of June, Frederick came to pick up Slewpy's Star to take her home. The mare in ICU had died, but her foal and the teaser were back at home and healthy. He and his wife had spent $40,000 in about a month.

Inside the admissions office, Barr went over her instructions on the discharge orders with Frederick while the barn crew went to get Slewpy's Star. Among other things, the mare would need aspirin once a day and the bandage around her abdomen, which covered the incision in her chest, removed in two days and left open. She'd also continue to get SLO twice a day for a while.

The two went out to Frederick's trailer. Outside, it was temperate; summer had not yet become stifling. The sky was sky-blue, the breeze soft. The barn crew loaded up the mare, and Barr watched as the trailer pulled out of the parking lot, past the other rigs, and the brown and white signs that say, "HORSES HAVE RIGHT OF WAY." "When they stay here that long, you get attached to them," she said to me before going back inside.

A month later, I accompanied Barr and Dr. Alexandra Tracey, an intern, when they visited the mare to evaluate her lungs and check to see if any fluid remained in her chest. It was the end of July and the grass and trees on the farm glowed green from the recent rain.

Slewpy's Star's residence is white, with a green-and-white sign reading "BROODMARE BARN."

The vet approached the stall; Slewpy's Star looked at her warily. "Look at you! Holy Smokes. You're fat!" said Barr. "I was here two weeks ago, and you weren't like this. I like it, I like it." The mare had more heft, especially in her heart girth. Although her mane was still dry and straggly, her coat was starting to gain luster.

"You almost look like a normal horse!" said Tracey.

Tracey set up the laptop for the ultrasound, and Barr moved in closer.

"The redhead's coming," Barr said to Slewpy's Star. "She's mean, she sticks things into me. You don't like me. I don't care as long as you're alive ..." The vet pressed her finger on the horse's neck, over part of the jugular vein, obstructing the blood flow for a moment. The segment of the vein above filled up with blood easily; it wasn't clotted, thick, and thready as before. "This vein's amazing!" said the vet.

Barr swabbed alcohol over Slewpy's Star's chest and did an ultrasound. The mare was continuing to heal. Her lungs looked healthy. There was a small pocket of fluid below the incision made for the endoscope, but the vet wasn't too worried. The horse hadn't been producing new fluid. Barr would recheck her in a couple of weeks and leave her on antibiotics until then.

We headed back to Rood & Riddle in Barr's red truck. For miles, we passed knots of mares and foals grazing on the sun-kissed day. "Look at these babies," said Tracey. "It reminds you they're not all sick."

As she drove, Barr mentioned that she'd had a case right before Slewpy's Star that was similar, a five-year-old chestnut mare, Faithful Enough (not her real name). She was a big, even-tempered Thoroughbred with a recent history of pleuropneumonia. She had developed an abscess that walled off in her chest; the abscess was so large, around the size of a small watermelon, it was pushing on her aorta, essentially causing a heart murmur. The owners had already spent a significant amount of money getting Faithful Enough through the pleuropneumonia. "They said, 'Let's just put her down,' " said Barr. "I couldn't do that." She thought, "This horse doesn't look that bad. We need to give her a chance." For the first time in Barr's career, she asked if she could have the horse. "My husband (a broodmare manager) said, 'You did what?' "

Barr didn't know about SLO at that time; Faithful Enough's treatment included daily draining and debriding. It took months, but the mare lived, got in foal by Flatter, a well-mannered son of top racing sire A.P. Indy, and had a colt in March 2008. She's the foundation broodmare at Barr and her husband's little farm. When I talked to Frederick later, he told me he'd heard about the case at the clinic,

Six months after she left the hospital, Slewpy's Star was healthy.

and that knowing Faithful Enough's owners had given up had made him want to try even harder. By the time Slewpy's Star left the hospital, her chart was 285 pages.

About five months after Slewpy's Star left Rood & Riddle, Dr. Peter Morresey used SLO as part of his treatment for a weanling with severe pneumonia. The weanling turned around. Morresey, like Barr, believes the drug may have played a role in the foal's recovery but wants to see more results.

The winter after Slewpy's Star returned home I went out to Oak Haven Farm for a visit. After talking with the Fredericks for about an hour, I went out to take a picture of the mare. She was in the front paddock, grazing with two pasture mates, both dark bays, she the only chestnut. She looked fit and solid, and her coat was a little dusty, as if she'd been rolling around in the dirt for fun. She was about 200 yards away. I called to her. She turned toward me, looking cross. She didn't move. I nickered, pleaded, and then begged since I knew no one was looking. Nothing. One of her pasture mates came a little closer and then stopped and looked at the chestnut mare as if asking for permission. Slewpy's Star looked at me irritably, a human who couldn't possibly know her mysteries, and then returned to her grass for a few minutes. Then she walked off, going as far away as she could to the other end of the paddock, where it was impossible to get a good picture. Slewpy's Star was well.

CHAPTER

13

Surely Awesome

A s Big Brown sped down the stretch to win the 2008 Kentucky Derby with Kent Desormeaux astride him, the two were one. (A good jockey, it is said, is "part horse" anyway.) After they won the Preakness by five and a half lengths, Desormeaux told a reporter, "I've been blessed with this freak of a horse."

As the Belmont approached, trainer Rick Dutrow assured everyone his horse would be the first to win the Triple Crown in three decades. But Big Brown didn't win. He faltered around the second turn, with Desormeaux easing him up. He came in last. Whether it was a shoe that wasn't secure, a hoof with an unhealed crack, exhaustion, or something else, nobody will ever know. That's the thing about a horse, and not just a Thoroughbred. Not one is a safe bet, for your money or your heart.

No case I saw at Rood & Riddle exemplified this more than that of Surely Awesome. In spring of 2008, the gentle, sorrel-colored Quarter Horse was at a farm in western Kentucky waiting to foal. Her owners, veterinarian Susan Blackburn and her family, live in upstate New York. Surely Awesome was in Kentucky because the

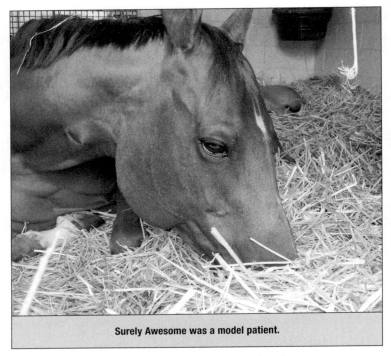

Surely Awesome was a model patient.

family was participating in an economic development program through the Kentucky Quarter Horse Association that awards incentives for breeding and foaling in the state.

Surely Awesome was thirteen years old and so was Blackburn's daughter, Juliana, who had learned to ride on the mare about three years earlier. While some horses take advantage of inexperienced riders, refusing to do what they want and acting out, with Juliana, Surely Awesome "never scared her, never cheated her," says Blackburn. Unlike other mares — grumpy one day, nice the next — Surely Awesome was consistent: sweet, willing, her ears always forward, her strongest desire to please her owners. Juliana and the mare won numerous competitions in various disciplines. But as Surely Awesome got older, she couldn't be as competitive. Blackburn and her husband, Bill Baskin, decided to keep the mare as a trail horse instead of selling her, afraid she would end up with an uncaring owner who might "show her like an automobile." They decided to breed her because they thought she would enjoy being a mother and that her foal might inherit her temperament.

At the farm in western Kentucky where she had been bred, Surely Awesome was a month away from foaling when she came in one night from the paddock limping, her right hind leg swollen. The farm's vet found that the mare had what's called a comminuted P1 fracture, meaning her long pastern bone was shattered. The pastern is made up of the bones, ligaments, and tendons located between the fetlock and the hoof. It acts as a shock absorber, and its length and angle are crucial to the strength and quality of a horse's gait. Blackburn believes the mare twisted the leg in a fence-post hole that wasn't properly filled.

Blackburn is a large and small animal veterinarian with a passion for horses. When she graduated from veterinary school at Tufts University in Massachusetts in the 1980s, she had been offered an internship at Rood & Riddle but was unable to take it for family reasons. Now, decades later, she didn't know if the clinic would be the place to send Surely Awesome for the best medical care. She called an equine veterinarian-friend in the Bluegrass for advice. "There's one place to go and one person to go to," he told her: Dr. Alan Ruggles at Rood & Riddle.

Ruggles is one of the top equine orthopedic surgeons in the country. He came to Rood & Riddle from Ohio State University, where he was an associate professor in clinical orthopedic surgery. Before that, he was at the University of Pennsylvania's New Bolton Center, one of the most highly regarded large animal veterinary teaching clinics in the world. Ruggles is in his mid-forties; I would vote him one of the veterinarians who would be most fun to take on a road trip. He tells good stories. He listens to Ted Nugent when he's doing surgery. When I rode with him, he drove fast (if a bit recklessly), asked for directions, and I am certain he would pull over if you wanted to check out a view or stop and eat at a roadside diner you spotted in the shape of a giant piece of fruit. The vet has thick gray and black hair, gray-blue eyes, and a beard when he feels like it. When I met him for the first time, as he was cutting open a foal that had a radial fracture, he said I could feel free to describe him as ruggedly handsome, and he actually is handsome, not in a conventional way but in a Spencer Tracy way: an Everyman face animated by a distinctive personality with a big emotional range. He grew up on Long Island, and was a groom, hot walker, and then veterinary assistant at Belmont and Saratoga racetracks from around nineteen years old to twenty-four. It's easy to imagine him as the favorite kid at the track, schmoozing with everyone from owners to exercise riders. He went to veterinary school at Cornell University with the help of a scholarship from the Horsemen's Benevolent and Protective Association, a group designed to help racetrack employees, along with financial help offered by some horse owners and businesspeople he met at the track who wanted him to succeed. Some people remember the stages and turning points of their lives by historic events, others by songs; for Ruggles it is racehorses, specifically, who won the Belmont in any given year. Say 1979 to him, for example, and he conjures up Coastal's upset of Spectacular Bid. Coastal was lightly raced and had vision problems; Spectacular Bid, a blue streak of a horse, was on track to become the next Triple Crown winner. It was the year of Ruggles' high school graduation, and he had to miss the race because of the ceremony.

But even with his fun nature, the vet's state of mind at work is often tied to how well his patients are doing, so it can go up and down. Some interns and barn crew find him gruff. Vets and staff who know him best say he always has your back and never gets aggravated without good reason — an IV cart missing something important in the middle of treating a tense and dangerous patient, for example, or the intern who clipped a yearling for a procedure after being told repeatedly not to, as it would ruin the coat for an upcoming sale.

It was after hours when the trailer arrived at Rood & Riddle with Surely Awesome. On the X-rays, the long pastern bone in her right hind leg was in so many pieces it was a "bag of ice," as such severe fractures are called around the clinic. The bone was in eight large pieces and ten little pieces, the skin crumpled around it. But as a rule, the lower the fracture, the better the chance there is of saving the horse. Also, Surely Awesome's bone had not broken through the skin.

An ultrasound showed the baby was healthy. Ruggles' plan was to do surgery and then hope the mare could both carry the baby to term and see her own pastern mend. Surely Awesome faced the danger of developing a secondary infection, such as a respiratory problem from lying down too much, or an infection of the placenta triggered by the stress of her situation, either of which could compromise the health of the foal.

The next day the mare was anesthetized and taken into surgery lying on her left side. Ruggles made an incision a little less than three inches down Surely Awesome's fetlock. Using forceps to hold two large pieces of the fracture together at the top of the pastern, Ruggles drilled in two bone screws to join them. Then two nearby fragments were joined by drilling in a single screw.

With the top of the pastern done, Ruggles headed for the bottom of the bone, which was cracked. Based on X-rays, he placed a drill bit in the approximate location of the crack to mark it. Then he took another set of digital X-rays, available in moments on a monitor in front of him. Using them as a guide, he made two small incisions and drilled two screws through them into the crack. The middle of the bone was in too many pieces to screw together. The goal was to stabilize the top and the bottom of the fracture, so the middle fragments would be aligned as they mended.

The vet closed the long pastern up. Next he put Surely Awesome in what's called a pin cast. Holes were drilled through the mare's cannon bone and two pins inserted horizontally. Then everything was wrapped with a sterile bandage, and a cast applied. Now every time Surely Awesome took a step, the weight would be transferred from the pastern to the cannon bone through the pins, letting the fractured pieces heal unstressed.

While recuperating, horses can't stay off their feet, lie in bed, watch soaps. When horses with injuries like Surely Awesome's run into trouble in recovery, it often isn't from the original injury but from secondary, sometimes deadly, complications such as laminitis, caused by too much pressure being put on the supporting limbs. The mare's left hind leg was particularly vulnerable.

Surely Awesome's three healthy feet were X-rayed to get a baseline in order to detect any signs of the disease that might surface in the future. Then her left hind foot was fitted with a special shoe, cushioned by dental impression material packed inside. The material had the consistency of window caulking and would help distribute the weight over a greater surface area of the hoof to help prevent one part from receiving more pressure than another.

Her surgery now completed and laminitis precautions taken, the mare took up residence in stall 1 of Barn 1, the home for trauma cases. Now everyone would just have to wait.

***

In the United States equine orthopedics is still a young field, less than fifty years old. Two factors helped lead to its growth in the late 1960s and '70s: the creation of board-certified specialties in veterinary education and advancements in equine anesthetic techniques, allowing veterinarians to keep a horse safely under long enough to do complex surgery. The 1970s forward saw advancement in fracture repair using screws and plates (pioneered in this country by the late Dr. Jacques Jenny at the New Bolton Center), as well as arthroscopy adapted from human techniques. (In the 1990s, implants, as the screws and plates are called, were especially designed for horses, an extremely important step in equine orthopedics.) Another key advancement came in 1978 with fetlock arthrodesis, pioneered by Rood & Riddle surgeon Larry Bramlage when he was at Ohio State. Fetlock injuries were the most common fatal injuries among racehorses before the procedure, which fuses the fetlock (for more, see Chapter 15). Bramlage and Ruggles are among a group of approximately 450 large animal surgeons in the country certified by the American College of Veterinary Surgeons, and part of an elite group of less than thirty who are not only nationally, but globally, known as the go-to veterinarians for horse orthopedics.

Expertise only comes with experiencing multiple cases. Given what he had seen in his career, Ruggles gave Surely Awesome a 50-50 chance of surviving, and a 70 percent chance if nothing went wrong in the first four weeks.

The month spent waiting to see if the mare could carry her baby to term passed slowly for the worried humans involved. Techs took her out to graze a bit to keep her from getting bored. Surely Awesome had always been cautious on concrete and stepped gingerly on the asphalt until she made it to the grass, where she seemed at ease. The X-rays showed the fracture was mending on schedule, and no signs of laminitis surfaced in her other feet. Roughly once each week, Dr. Bonnie Barr put an ultrasound to the mare's abdomen and looked at the fuzzy night of the screen to check the health of the fetus, timing its heart rate — too fast or too slow would indicate stress — and making sure there were enough fetal fluids, and that the placenta and uterus were healthy. The foal looked well, although it was impossible for the ultrasound to catch everything.

As the baby got heavier, Surely Awesome was found lying down more. However, she was managing better than other mares the hospital staff had seen in similar situations: She had been in good physical condition before the accident and had the personality to handle stress — mellow and patient. She liked her medical team, and when they scratched her withers she scratched their shoulders back with her muzzle, never nipping with her teeth, as if she knew that would hurt.

Dr. Eric Carlson was the vet on call the night Surely Awesome foaled. It was 2 a.m. on a Friday, four weeks after the mare arrived, when he got a message on his cell phone that she was starting to foal. He ran down to her stall.

Surely Awesome was standing, and part of the chorioallantois, one of the two membranes that make up the placenta, was hanging from the lips of the mare's vulva. It was a bad sign — the placenta had prematurely separated from the uterus; the foal wasn't getting the oxygen it needed. It was an emergency. The scenario is called a red bag delivery because the chorioallantois is red. No one knows exactly why red bags occur. In Surely Awesome's case it could have been from the stress of having such a severe injury while pregnant.

Carlson quickly opened up the placenta. The foal, to his relief, was in the normal position for delivery, head and feet first. He put the canvas obstetrical straps on the foal's legs to help pull it out. Surely Awesome lay down as soon as he put them on, as if she wanted to help.

Carlson pulled on the straps. The baby slipped out easily. It was a filly, the color of dark honey. Her nostrils were cleared and vitals signs checked; they were all good. The vet clamped and cut her umbilical cord and swabbed her navel with antiseptic. A healthy foal was on the ground.

***

Ruggles' nine-year-old daughter nicknamed the foal Sophie. She was a joyful filly, and liked to run around the stall she shared with her mom kicking up her hind legs. Blackburn decided to keep the baby with the mom instead of sending her to a nursemare at a local farm. It was a difficult decision because that would mean the foal would be cooped up in the stall, possibly becoming underdeveloped. But it was too hard to monitor a foal's physical and mental well-being with a nursemare from so far away. Because of the mare's equanimity, neither Blackburn nor Ruggles thought the foal would put stress on Surely Awesome by nursing.

When Sophie was a week old, on a Saturday in June, Blackburn and her family came down from New York to visit. I got to Rood & Riddle shortly before they arrived. On the stall door were two fluorescent pink stickers: "MORE BEDDING" and then the same thing in Spanish: "MAS PACA," meaning the stall required extra straw to cushion the mare when she was down to reduce the possibility of bedsores.

Sophie was dozing in the hay. She stretched and swished her tail. Surely Awesome stood watching over her. Her right hind fetlock was in the purple pin cast, her other legs wrapped in green "standing bandages" to provide additional support. The mare shifted her weight from one back leg to the other as I watched. While I waited I started talking to a tech in the barn. As he gave Surely Awesome more water, I commented on how she seemed to be doing well so far. He was quiet and then said before leaving: "The worry is always with the other leg."

Blackburn came up to the stall with her husband and daughter. Her shoulder-length blonde hair glinted in the sun filtering through the stall window. She wore a shirt the color of a red bandanna. She peered through the grate at the mare. "Oh, Schnoodle," she said.

In one hand, Juliana held a stack of photos to show me of her in horse shows on Surely Awesome. In her other hand was a jumbo bag of organic carrots. Blackburn's husband, Bill, quietly brought up the rear.

We talked while waiting for Ruggles. As a veterinarian, Blackburn was in the position of going back and forth between her calm professional self and her emotional, mother-of-the-patient self. Knowing every possible outcome was comforting intellectually and worrisome emotionally. She summed it up: "We're by no means out of the woods ... not a lot of people would have spent the money but it was either save her or kill both of them." (Many veterinarians casually use the word "kill" instead of saying euthanize, in the same way human emergency room doctors use slang with each other like NGMI — "not gonna make it.")

"When you show a horse, you spend so much time with them," she went on. "When Juliana was little, I did most of the work: bathing, grooming, saddling. It's like a child. You get attached to them."

Her husband turned toward the stall. Surely Awesome was still at the far end with her rump toward us. "I'm surprised she hasn't come down to the gate."

"It's painful for her to turn around," said Blackburn. The foal got up and started to nurse. "What do you think of yourself?" Blackburn said to Sophie.

When Ruggles showed up, Blackburn commented that Surely Awesome looked well-fed. Ruggles agreed, saying she didn't look like she'd been raised by wolves. "She's gaining weight," Ruggles said. "But the problem is getting her enough activity." He told Blackburn the mare was getting a rub at the top of her cast, so he had cut the cast back down instead of changing it. The skin would heal, he said, and it was important to keep the pin cast on as long as possible.

Ruggles opened the stall door and led Surely Awesome out for a short walk of about six to eight feet back and forth in front of the stall. Even though she walked stiffly and carefully, like someone with bad arthritis or a new knee, Blackburn was pleased.

"I tell you, she walks better than I thought she would," said Blackburn.

"It got immensely better after she had the foal," said Ruggles.

"You're happy with how the healing is progressing?" asked Blackburn.

"Well, you won't have much healing until the pin cast is off," said Ruggles. We headed over to radiology where we looked at the X-rays on the light stand. He pointed at the fracture. "It's healing, but the mineralization isn't happening. It's basically in traction right now." It would take sixteen weeks for the bone to heal. Right now it was "bone jelly." Once the fracture was stable enough to bear weight, Surely Awesome would come out of the pin cast into a regular cast.

Ruggles explained the surgery to the family. Pointing at the X-rays, he showed how he put in one screw after another.

"It's like drawing a graph; this point, this point, and this point," said Ruggles.

"Woodworking 101," said Blackburn.

"Glorified mechanic; that's what my mom says," replied Ruggles.

The mare would likely have a shortened limb when she healed, and would need to wear a special shoe for life to extend her hoof. One long-term concern was arthritis. To prevent it, Ruggles had been careful to align the joint surfaces in surgery, but any infection now could cause damage and improper healing, resulting in arthritis. If that happened, the mare likely would require a second surgery to fuse her fetlock, and going back in always brings risk.

The family prepared to leave. Blackburn stood behind Juliana holding her shoulders. "She watched Barbaro, watched the whole thing," she said, referring to the 2006 Kentucky Derby winner who broke down in the Preakness. His recovery at the New Bolton Center was followed by millions of people, thousands of whom sent trucks of get-well cards as well as things like holy water from Rome and a Christmas tree made of apples. After eight months, Barbaro had to be put down because of laminitis. Ruggles had been a resident under Dean Richardson, Barbaro's doctor, and the two men were now not only colleagues but golf buddies.

"It's different, yet the same," said Ruggles. Barbaro had also injured his right hind leg, but it had been much worse than Surely Awesome's: In addition to a long pastern bone shattered in twenty pieces and a dislocated fetlock, he had a broken sesamoid bone behind his ankle, and a condylar fracture of the cannon bone (the condyle is the bulb-shaped end of the cannon bone that fits into the fetlock joint). However, Surely Awesome had the same threat of infection and laminitis as Barbaro did in recovery. Ruggles looked at Surely Awesome's X-ray again. "The bone is getting stronger from stress. In time it will fill in. It's pretty amazing."

The bone would remodel itself (repair and strengthen) through time and exercise. It would never be pretty, but that didn't matter. This change in the bone's internal architecture, as Ruggles called it, through the intelligence of the body (whether in horses or people) never stopped fascinating him. Yet although that process was straightforward, it didn't mean the healing would be. As Ruggles told me once: "Nothing is uneventful, even if it's uncomplicated."

The year before, in 2007, Ruggles had a client who brought in a Standardbred colt — call the horse Sixer — with a hairline fracture on his long pastern bone, nothing too severe. After surgery to place two screws to stabilize the fracture, he was doing nicely at Rood & Riddle. It looked like he would be able to race again. But the problem with fractures such as Sixer's is that although his was a vertical crack down the bone, the possibility of a virtually invisible horizontal crack existed, one impossible to see on X-rays. Ten X-rays were shot of Sixer's injury, but no horizontal crack was apparent. Shortly after leaving the hospital to recover with his trainer, he was found in his stall with the bone shattered. He could have kicked the wall, or a stealth crack could have triggered it. Yet after a second surgery with bone plates and screws, Sixer eventually did mend. Now, he's at stud. Two years earlier, a Standardbred mare came in with an injury similar to Surely Awesome's, and she, too, recovered. Yet there were also the horses with P1 fractures who didn't make it, like Sailing, whose picture hangs on one of the walls at the hospital. Sailing was a big Irish draft sport horse, a laid-back champion who shattered his long pastern while up near Chicago. After months in recovery at Rood & Riddle, with everything going smoothly, a bone infection developed that could not be resolved, and he had to be euthanized.

About two and a half weeks after Surely Awesome's surgery, I went out with Ruggles on a couple of farm calls. "These are difficult cases," he said in reference to Blackburn's mare and foal. He seemed worried. "The goal has always been to save both of them, but the mare's progress isn't too spiffy ... She's got an abscess close to her joint. I took the cast off Saturday and put her in a splint, but she needs to be back in the cast. Now, it's a soft tissue problem." He was worried Surely Awesome might put greater stress on the opposite hind foot, increasing the possibility of laminitis. "I'd love to get her in a (regular) cast this week."

"It wears you out if you lose a horse like her," Ruggles said, "You've invested so much."

During the drive we also talked about what he considers the biggest advances in equine medicine in the last ten years. One of them is the locking compression plate for fractures, a development that came from human medicine. Instead of using regular screws to attach steel plates to fractures, the new plates allow screws to lock into them. "It's like a splint that's under the skin, so it's extremely strong; it's very hard for the screws to come out," said Ruggles. Such a plate was used to repair Barbaro's right hind limb. Another advance Ruggles mentioned is the use of MRI for horses, which generates a more detailed, cross-sectional image of a limb, joint, or foot than regular X-rays and ultrasound. For example, with MRI Ruggles can see the extent of an infection in a foal's joint in great depth and whether the infection has gone into bone. I asked if he believes the future holds the possibility of owners putting their racehorses in the MRI as a precautionary measure to try to identify vulnerable bones and avoid breakdowns. "Not right now," he said, "but perhaps down the road." Structural or physical changes in bones may one day be identified as precursors to serious fractures, he said, but a lot of data has to be collected and analyzed before that's possible. Owners would also have to be willing to have the horse put under general anesthesia for the procedure. Other new science into preventing racing breakdowns includes Colorado State University's research into biomarkers for muskoskeletal disease or bone problems. The biomarkers — indicators of damage — are detected through a blood test; for example, in one experiment, horses with tendon or ligament injuries had a measurable increase in the level of a bone-specific type of collagen.

At the end of the farm calls, Ruggles told me about a recent dinner party he attended where the guests included a pediatric oncologist and a car dealer. The latter said to the former, "Doc, you have a lot of pressure in your job, huh?" Yes, the doctor replied. The car dealer looked at him and said, in all seriousness: "Twenty cars on the lot at the end of the month. Now *that's* pressure, doc." Four days later, Ruggles found the abscess wasn't in Surely Awesome's joint; a regular cast went on her right hind leg, and she started doing better. But not long after, X-rays showed laminitis developing in the mare's left hind foot. However, many horses recover when the disease is caught early. The left hind leg went into a cast now too. As the days passed Surely Awesome stayed stable and seemed to be mending all-around. Three weeks later, she and Sophie went to a hospital barn owned by a Rood & Riddle employee and her husband. It was important for the foal to get out in the paddock; she was undersized from confinement as had been Blackburn's concern, and needed exercise and sunshine. Ruggles thought the mare could be monitored at the lay-up barn, with him making regular visits. But the pressure was still on for the vet, less pressure, to be honest, than being the physician of a child with cancer, but more pressure, of course, than the car dealer with twenty sedans left to unload on the last day of the month. In two and half months Surely Awesome had made it this far, and her owners kept praying she could go the whole way.

***

In one account of Greek mythology, man was created by Prometheus, the shrewd Titan, and his flighty brother, Epimetheus. Epimetheus started the process, but he first "gave all the best gifts to the animals, strength and swiftness and courage and shrewd cunning, fur and feathers and wings and shells and the like — until no good was left for men ... no quality to make them a match for the beasts." Prometheus then stepped in. He shaped man in a "nobler" form than animals, stood him on two feet, and handed him fire. All this was supposed to make man "superior" to any creature.

However, as I followed Surely Awesome's case, it was hard for me to believe that any man or woman could be called superior in temperament to the mare. Reviewing the facts: Her leg had been catastrophically broken while she was pregnant and she had undergone major surgery. During recovery, she carried the baby to term and then nursed it. Then she developed laminitis in her other leg; the dangerous inflammation of the laminae put her in constant pain. She had been living in a space the size of a large bathroom for months, with the equine version of a toddler who actually kicked her at least twice, once in the bad leg, another time in the left front (causing no serious damage to either, fortunately). Yet the entire time, the mare had never been anything but pleasant to everybody.

Still, once Surely Awesome got to the hospital barn, similar to a rehab facility for humans, she seemed a little more relaxed than she had been at Rood & Riddle, according to barn owners Bruce and Kaye Kincaid. Just as humans find hospitals depressing, so do horses. Now Surely Awesome was in a more natural setting, away from other sick horses and the medicalization of her life, and she and her foal were turned out twice daily for about an hour and a half. It wasn't as long as a healthy horse's turnout, and the mare couldn't roam freely — she had her own part of the paddock that was sectioned off to restrict her exercise, reducing the chances of injury — but it was one more step toward normalcy.

But as the days passed, the mare started lying down a bit more. Sometimes, the foal nursed from her as she rested on her side. Yet she still seemed to be stable according to her X-rays. It was now early August, about three and a half months since the fracture. Ruggles had a vacation planned, but was reluctant to go. "I hate going on vacation; something always happens," he told Kaye Kincaid.

Laminitis can quickly turn serious, and if something did happen with the mare, it would happen fast, he told her. He was correct. He visited Surely Awesome on a Wednesday, and on Thursday, en route with his family to Chicago, and then onto Wisconsin, he got a call from Rood & Riddle veterinarian Dr. Vern Dryden. Dryden works in the hospital's podiatry department and was the staff member overseeing Surely Awesome's feet.

So many stories in the horse world are about missed chances or almost making it — the colt that almost won the big race like his grand-sire. The mare that had just about recovered from a difficult delivery but then died of an infection. The thousands of shocked people in the stands right after the Belmont; two minutes earlier they had thought Big Brown would win the Triple Crown. It is this *almostness* that can drive you crazy, whether you're in breeding, racing, training, owning, showing, healing. Surely Awesome had almost made it.

New X-rays taken by Dryden showed the coffin bone in the mare's left hind foot had started to rotate. The laminae had broken down, allowing the bone to sink from the weight of her standing on it. The pain had to be excruciating. The rotation would continue, and eventually the bone would come through the bottom of the foot. Her whole hoof capsule was set to come off — the slang phrase is her feet were about to fall off. On the right hind leg, the screws were coming out of the fracture from the pressure of the mare favoring the injured leg. She needed to be euthanized. In short, she did not mend fast enough on the bad leg to take the pressure off the good one.

Ruggles called Blackburn from Wisconsin and told her the news.

"If you need me to come home to be the one to put her to sleep, I'll do it," the vet said. Blackburn didn't want to ruin the vacation for Ruggles' family.

Blackburn told him, "I told everybody in my family all along, 'Until she walks off the trailer, don't get your hopes up.' But I forgot to listen to myself."

"So did I," Ruggles replied.

On Sunday, Dr. Travis Tull, Rood & Riddle's surgical resident, came out to the Kincaids' farm. He sedated Sophie heavily and then walked Surely Awesome out to the grass and euthanized her. The following month, Sophie would go back to New York to Blackburn and her family. But that night in Kentucky, and the week after, Sophie appeared to alternate between sad and mad. Some days, she would wheel around and try to kick people; others, she would nicker and ask for play and a rub more than usual. After a while, she seemed to reach an equilibrium; she looked for connection elsewhere, whether it was in people or the barn cat. A bay gelding on the farm also took her under his wing. But for weeks, she would walk into the part of the paddock that had been sectioned off for Surely Awesome and stand there; she could still catch the mare's scent. Six months later, Blackburn's grief over the mare remained ever-present. The box sent back from Kentucky shortly after Surely Awesome died containing the mare's halter and other things sat in the back hall of her house. Blackburn could not open it.

CHAPTER

14

Worries

It was a spring afternoon in 2001, and Tom Riddle, the clinic's co-founder, was out fetal-sexing mares, examining them to determine the gender of the foal in utero. It's a difficult procedure that few people know how to do, and it took him two years to learn. Except for the unusual weather — record-warm temperatures followed by frost and then drought — it was an ordinary spring for the Bluegrass horse world. Riddle palpated one of the six mares he was there to see, and the uterus felt normal for a fetus between sixty and seventy days gestation, the swelling about the size of a football. Then he inserted the ultrasound probe. The screen of the small beige box, however, revealed the fetus was dead, surrounded by a strange, cloudy fluid. Same thing with another fetus. He thought it was unusually bad luck for the farm to find two dead babies on the same day. The year before, out of 400 mares he had fetal-sexed, only five fetuses were dead.

The next day, Riddle went out to another farm in a completely different part of the Bluegrass to fetal-sex six more mares. Again, two fetuses dead. Now the veterinarian was worried about an illness affecting the foal population. Three days later, another dead baby in another county. He started asking around, but other vets told him they had not seen early foal losses. The next day, after finding three more deaths, Riddle contacted the state diagnostic lab and the University of Kentucky's Gluck Equine Research Center. Riddle's discovery was the beginning of the most devastating health crisis ever to strike the Bluegrass Thoroughbred world: Mare Reproductive Loss Syndrome. By the time the worst of the plague was over, at the end of 2001, 550 late-term foals were dead, and between 2,000 and 3,000 mares had aborted in early pregnancy. (The losses weren't limited to Thoroughbreds but included other breeds; 2002 saw over 750 foal deaths.) Riddle, a shy and retiring individual, was forced into the public spotlight as the equine veterinarian who not only sounded the alarm on MRLS, but documented its unfolding for the country through media interviews with every major news organization.

"How many more am I going to lose? Am I going to survive this?" These were the questions farm and horse owners wanted to know from Riddle and other equine veterinarians. Reporters from publications such as the *New York Times*, *National Geographic*, *U.S. News and World Report*, and *Sports Illustrated* wanted to know what Riddle was seeing and if any solution was pending. Riddle was finding necrosing fetuses sixty to eighty days old in the cervix, vagina, and vulva, when typically a mare expels an early pregnancy within two days, and vets don't ever see it. In the late-term pregnancies, foals were being born dead or close to it, unresponsive, unable to stand up. At the Livestock Diagnostic Center, foal corpses were stacked on top of each other three and four feet high. As far as when and if MRLS would end, "No one knew," says Riddle today. "We didn't have any history to fall back on."

In the epidemiological detective story, by the end of May 2001 University of Kentucky researchers had begun to link the deaths to mares ingesting Eastern tent caterpillars, which nest in wild cherry trees that surround the Bluegrass and its farms. The caterpillar is black with yellow and white racing stripes down its back; it was first reported seen in the United States in the 1600s. The caterpillars may have had a longer life cycle in spring of 2001 because of the unusual weather. The same weather pattern in the early 1980s had produced a slew of similar foal deaths, but not in as large numbers. Researchers first believed the deaths were caused by cyanide from the cherry trees, whose sugars can produce the toxin under specific conditions. The theory was the caterpillars were ingesting the toxin and then carrying it to horses. However, later research linked the deaths to the caterpillar's fuzzy pelt, which has thousands of little hairs believed to puncture a mare's alimentary tract, allowing bacteria from the tract to then access and harm a fetus and the placenta.

Farm owners cut down trees, sprayed others with insecticides, and kept mares out of pastures bordered by them and any other host foliage. However, economic damage to the horse industry came to nearly $336 million in 2001 alone. By the 2003 foaling season, the syndrome had for the most part passed. The weather pattern in 2001 that appeared to trigger the crisis has not recurred, but farm managers and other horse people remain constantly on guard today for signs of the caterpillar and MRLS. In 2008, experts found the highest numbers of caterpillars seen in the Bluegrass since 2001 because of a cooler spring, but the syndrome did not strike again.

Regardless of the presence of MRLS, numerous farm managers I met over the year continuously fret about the health of their horses and the possibility of problems such as paddock accidents. Equine vets are the recipients of such anxieties and they are also the first to get vented on if, say, a mare isn't pregnant, or the sex of the foal isn't what a client wants.

Says Riddle, "My reaction to their worry is just to remain calm; you try and be reassuring. That doesn't mean I'm not worried inside, too. I try and be positive and optimistic, and by nature, I am. It puts me in a good position to try and reassure them that we're going to be all right. … I liken the veterinarian's position quite often to that of a coach of an athletic team. When your team is winning, everybody is happy and you're a great guy. But things start to go wrong, the client, like the fans, can get down on the veterinarian, like a coach, and you have to prepare for that and realize there are some things beyond your control, and concentrate on things you do have control over."

It was a relief for Riddle when the media storm and MRLS eventually ended and he could get back to his job as a horse gynecologist, checking on the status of broodmares' pregnancies or the state of their fertility. Riddle is 6 foot 2, quiet, with a black beard scattered with gray. Clients, colleagues, and friends describe him as a man with no guile and the type of person you find at a party checking out the host's bookshelves in the den instead of joining the crowd in the kitchen. Riddle talks carefully, as carefully as he palpates prized mares, going through the same steps every time, never varying, never impatient. However, after being around him for a while, you find that underneath the seal of his carefulness exists a wicked sense of humor. It appears in the dry-witted remark that surfaces out of nowhere, like a penny glinting on the sidewalk.

The life of an equine vet is one that Riddle never thought he'd follow his father into — the elder Riddle had a veterinary practice fifteen yards from his family's Greenville, South Carolina, house. Dr. Herbert Riddle did the large animal work, a partner the small animal. Tom Riddle helped out with both practices upon parental orders, reluctantly, he told me, because it always cut into his free time. His parents would have to tell friends who called or came by things like, "Thomas can't go out. He's with a cancerous cat right now."

However, his father also leased a stable to a Saddlebred trainer, and it was there Tom Riddle developed a great love for horses. He went into college as a pre-med student, but away at school found himself missing horses. He started thinking about veterinary school, and that if he had a practice focused solely on equines — no cows with foot rot or poodles with ear infections — it would be different from his growing up. Riddle got accepted both to medical school and veterinary school, and wrestled with the decision for a long time before going with the latter. (Various vets I talked to during my year at the clinic faced a similar dilemma in college.)

Even with Riddle's love for the work and his financial success, it is a demanding life. From January through June when it is Thoroughbred foaling and breeding season, Riddle is up at 4 a.m. seven days a week, asleep by 9 p.m. He hates the cold, and the barns are miserably damp and freezing in winter. Although Riddle is home in time for dinner almost every night, it is not a job that you ever turn off. The other day, while cleaning out his desk at home, he found an old ultrasound picture he'd saved of a fetus. He was excited, thinking it

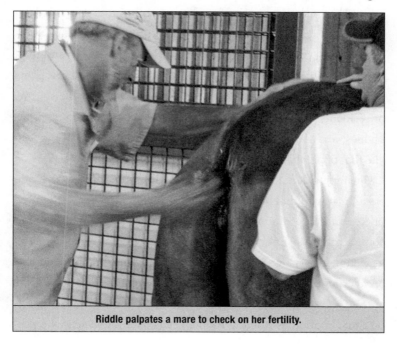

Riddle palpates a mare to check on her fertility.

was a picture of one of his three grown kids in utero. The image was of a foal out of Winning Colors, one of the three fillies to win the Kentucky Derby. (Winning Colors was also the horse who gave Riddle the worst kick of his life, catching the back of his thigh during a rectal palpation. She didn't break his leg, but the pain and the bruises stayed for weeks. The roan mare died in 2008 at twenty-three.)

But when I accompanied Riddle on a farm call one summer day, I realized the draw of being an equine veterinarian, at least one in the field, no matter how consuming the job or how ever-present the possibility of getting kicked. It was late August; the weather was clear, no humidity, a flirty breeze. As we drove, miles of blue sky and green pastures unfurled before us. The landscape made me remember what an acquaintance's niece, flying into Lexington for the first time, said when she looked out the window of her plane: "I've never seen so many shades of green." As we turned into the driveway, Riddle said, "These are the kind of farms that remind me of my dad." It was a small spread. The barn was black with white trim, and worn bridles hung from a row of hooks near the entrance. A handful of horses lived there. The family was excited to hear the foal was going to be a colt. The only other sounds were birdsongs and the shifting of residents in their stalls. Away from texting, computers and cell phones, and the news of a troubled economy, Riddle's job seemed like that of an old-fashioned country vet in another era.

Having just left a big city, I also thought on that day, and on others after it with different vets, about how calming it is to be around horses and other animals, how peaceful they can be and how uncomplicated. Most horses are patient. Most people are not. For college students trying to decide whether to go into human medicine or veterinary, those facts can contribute to making a choice for the latter. Then of course, there's always one of the big reasons Dr. Katie Garrett, another Rood & Riddle veterinarian, told me why people choose to become doctors of equines rather than of humans: "Patients look a lot better with their clothes off."

One summer morning I drove with Riddle out to Woodford Thoroughbreds, a commercial broodmare farm in Versailles, Kentucky, where the vet would fetal-sex a seventeen-year-old mare named Turko's Turn. Since the start of her broodmare career, including the MRLS years, Turko's Turn has been a solid producer, as a mare that births strong, healthy babies every year is called in the horse industry. (By virtue of her foaling dates and breeding schedules in 2001 and 2002, she was not exposed to MRLS.) However, her last several years had been full of drama, including the loss of a foal for the first time.

Turko's Turn is a large chestnut mare with soulful brown eyes. She's sweet-tempered, but likes regularity and structure, and gets nervous without it. She is the mother of Point Given, the only Thoroughbred ever to win four million-dollar races in a row: the Preakness Stakes, Belmont Stakes, Haskell Invitational, and Travers Stakes in 2001. That same year, Turko's Turn was voted Broodmare of the Year. In 2008, one of her yearlings sold for $1.2 million. Riddle has been Turko's Turn's doctor for six years, a time period over which he says he's developed a solid connection with his patient as well as real affection.

Turko's Turn is a daughter of champion Turkoman, and a granddaughter of Alydar, another acclaimed racehorse and stallion whose death figured in one of the best-known Shakespearean tales of the Bluegrass horse world: the failure of Calumet Farm, which was one of the most successful Thoroughbred farms in the region from the early 1930s to the late 1960s. Alydar was euthanized in 1990 after he broke his leg a second time after surgery to repair it. (The surgery was performed by Calumet chief vet Dr. William Baker and Rood & Riddle's Dr. Larry Bramlage.) The farm's owner at that time, J.T. Lundy, had driven the farm into the ground financially. Rumors abounded that Alydar's leg had been intentionally broken the first time in order to collect insurance money, although it has never been proven, and, given the accident-prone nature of horses, no one will ever know what happened. Lundy was eventually convicted of fraud and served time in prison.

Turko's Turn's bad luck started in 2006 when she gave birth to a colt by a veteran sire named Gone West. It died three months after it was born from a joint infection. In 2007 she was in foal to the celebrity stallion Storm Cat, delivered the baby, quickly got in foal by Storm Cat again, and then, at ninety days pregnant, had one of the most dramatic colics anyone I know has ever heard about.

Dr. Bruce Howard, an ambulatory vet at the clinic, happened to be at Woodford filling in for Riddle, checking on broodmares, when the colic occurred. He was finishing up in another barn when he was called to the emergency. When he arrived, Turko's Turn was sweating and in extreme pain. Handlers were trying to walk her up and down the aisle, but the mare kept trying to lie down and roll. Howard sedated the mare and gave her painkillers, but they didn't alleviate her distress. Howard was able to reflux her, but virtually nothing came out, signifying her problem was probably along the lines of a large colon displacement or a twist.

Matt Lyons, the general manager of Woodford Thoroughbreds, grew up on a farm in western Ireland and has seen all number of equine medical crises, but he had never seen a mare in such agony. Turko's Turn quickly worsened, moving into a cycle of rising and then throwing herself down on the barn floor. Then she threw herself down violently and didn't move. Howard rushed over with his stethoscope and listened to her heart. He didn't hear a sound. Howard looked up at Lyons. "Matt, I think she just died," he said. Lyons was unglued.

While still listening to her heart, Howard pressed his knee to the mare's chest, performing cardiac compression. He heard a heartbeat … and then it stopped. He did it again. One more beat, then nothing. Howard said to one of the men in the barn, "Come over here, and do this [compression]," while he ran to his truck and got the drugs epinephrine to stimulate her heart and prednisolone sodium succinate for shock. He ran back, administered the drugs, continued the cardiac compression, and within five minutes that felt like twenty, heartbeats began stringing themselves together. The mare's intermittent gasping breaths that Howard had originally thought were death throes moved into regular breathing.

Howard, Lyons, farm manager Kirt Cahill, and the others there knew they had to get the mare to the hospital for emergency surgery but didn't know how. She weighed roughly 1,400 pounds and they didn't have a hoist in the barn, or a truck with a winch. Then the mare started to become more aware of her surroundings, the sedation wearing off. After they were sure her heartbeat was steady, they were able to roll her up onto her chest. In a few more minutes, with some urging, clucking, and a light slap, they were able to get her up and loaded into a waiting trailer.

Turko's Turn made it to the hospital alive and was rushed to surgery where Dr. Alan Ruggles found a large colon displacement and a twist, which he corrected. She remained pregnant, but there was great concern that she might lose the pregnancy down the road as a result of the experience. After six days at the clinic, Turko's Turn was well enough to go home. In 2008 she delivered a healthy Storm Cat colt, and one month later, she colicked severely again. This time, however, her heart didn't stop. Rushed again to the hospital, her surgeon was Dr. Brett Woodie, who found a twist in her large colon and fixed it. After five days, the mare went home. Soon after, she was bred to sire Distorted Humor, whose foal she was carrying when I met her in August 2008 with Riddle.

Turko's Turn looks serene early in her pregnancy.

It's hard to know exactly why Turko's Turn colicked so severely. In general, as discussed, the design of a horse's intestinal tract predisposes it to all sorts of problems because of, among other reasons, its size, complexity, and mobility. Some horses are simply more prone to colic than others. As Riddle set up his ultrasound to begin the fetal-sexing procedure, Lyons and Cahill recalled the mare's trials of the past few years.

For Thoroughbred farms, fetal-sexing is important because it helps determine their financial bottom line. In the United States, far more than in Europe, colts are considered stronger and faster than fillies, and so, in general, more valuable. Whether that is actually true depends on who you ask and how long you want to argue about it. Colts cost roughly 20 percent to 25 percent more at yearling sales in the United States, and colts have overwhelmingly, as mentioned, won the Kentucky Derby, a longed-for goal of so many people buying them.

Still, plenty of people believe fillies are as fast as colts, and as I wrote this chapter, super filly Rachel Alexandra won the Kentucky Oaks by more than twenty lengths, the widest margin since 1910. Her jockey, Calvin Borel, called her the number one Thoroughbred in the country, male or female, and she went on to win the 2009 Preakness. Colt or filly, what makes the Thoroughbred business unique from any other, as Riddle says, is that "all your hopes and dreams are placed on a living creature."

But back to more practical matters, some farms consider a colt a better investment because he has the potential to sire over 100 foals a year, while a broodmare can produce just one. Because Turko's Turn is an older broodmare who has already produced good colts, the farm would welcome a filly to carry on the bloodlines.

The fetal-sexing procedure Riddle was about to do was discovered by accident by a young vet student named Sandy Curran in the mid-1980s at the University of Wisconsin at Madison. She was actually simultaneously getting her DVM and a master's degree in reproductive physiology. For the latter, she was doing lab work for Dr. O.J. Ginther, the veterinarian and veterinary professor whose lab in the early '80s revolutionized how ultrasound technology could be used to study and assess large-animal reproduction.

Curran, who decided she wanted to be a vet in seventh grade after reading the James Herriot books, was working on a project for Ginther using ultrasound to study embryo development in cattle. She noticed she could figure out whether the developing fetus was male or female by the location on the ultrasound image of what's called its genital tubercle when the fetus was in a particular position. The tubercle is the embryonic structure that grows into either a clitoris or penis.

"I thought, 'Wouldn't it be cool if you could use ultrasound to determine the gender?' " said Curran when I interviewed her. Ginther and she pursued the project first for bovine use and then equine.

One thing led to another, and today Curran is something of a fetal-sexing veterinary celebrity. She has been everywhere from France to Brazil, teaching and giving presentations on the procedure, used on both equines and cattle. (Her current veterinary practice in Wisconsin specializes in the reproductive care of dairy cattle.)

"I never went looking for anything … I just walked into it," says Curran. "It was exciting. I don't think I realized the impact of it until I was asked to speak all over the world."

The trick to fetal-sexing is both to correctly position the ultrasound probe for the picture and then know how to interpret the image. When Riddle showed me Turko's Turn's ultrasound picture, it looked, as Curran said it does for most people at first, like "black-and-white mush." Then Riddle showed me how the infinitesimal tubercle, in the shape of a backward letter C, was located behind the developing hind limbs and below the tailhead, instead of between the legs or slightly in front of them. The mare was carrying a filly.

As the filly inside Turko's Turn grew, I kept in touch with Lyons on how the mare was doing. Turko's Turn progressed with her pregnancy with no colics or other problems through Halloween and winter. Still, Riddle was concerned about her throughout the year. I came by and visited once before spring, and Lyons told me the night watchman was doing everything but shining a flashlight on her to make sure she was still breathing during her sleep. Even so, Lyons himself is actually much more relaxed about his job than other people I met in charge of horse farms: "You try and manage as many aspects as you can; if [something bad] happens it happens. You do what you can, and leave the rest in the hands of the gods."

Spring came, and although everything was going well with Turko's Turn, I also started to worry about her, probably after seeing so many dystocias coming into the hospital. Then I started thinking about all the horse people and farm managers across the Bluegrass fretting about all the things that could happen to their mares and foals-in-waiting: those caterpillars with their dangerous hairy pelts; heart-stopping colics coming out of nowhere; groundhog holes lying in wait for slender ankles; roving opossums carrying EPM. It was just too much to think about, all those worries covering the Bluegrass like dandelions after rain. When I went to see Lyons right before Turko's Turn was scheduled to foal in early May, I asked him how he stayed so calm. He was sanguine on the fresh spring day, as Turko's Turn stood resplendent outside with her swollen middle, a Botticelli broodmare in the late-afternoon sun. "You can't lose sleep over it. Whatever will be will be."

A week or so later, Turko's Turn foaled on a Wednesday night around dinnertime. Lyons called me and I got there right afterward. The foaling went easily. The newborn filly sat up in the corner of the stall. She was a big girl, caramel colored, with a white blaze rolled

Turko's Turn gets some rest after successfully foaling a filly.

down the middle of her face. She looked a little dazed, as if she wasn't quite sure what this place was all about. Turko's Turn lay on her side next to her; she wasn't ready to get up. Her big chestnut frame rose and fell with her breathing. Her placenta was passing from the uterus correctly. The mare might stay there for a couple of hours, Lyons said, and that was fine. He's seen mares jump up right after foaling, start cramping, and then go into a severe colic. Turko's Turn needed a good rest, and she deserved it. As the foal looked around the stall, Lyons said, "Maybe you'll be the next Rachel Alexandra." Riddle was relieved when he heard about the problem-free birth.

A week later, I came with Riddle out to do a post-foaling check-up on the mare. He palpated Turko's Turn and then looked through a speculum at her cervix. Some urine was pooling at the bottom. The scenario sometimes happens with an older mare whose uterus isn't as toned as a younger one after birth. The weight of the uterus forces the vagina down at an angle, and when the mare urinates, the liquid collects around the cervix. Rest and medication would likely clear up the problem in a week or so, Riddle said. The foal had been taken from her mother and put on a nursemare. The farm believed the stress of nursing might trigger another colic in Turko's Turn, who, at her age, isn't as resilient as she used to be. If everything went well, the farm was going to try and get her in foal again within a month, starting a new cycle in the business of breeding. I can't help but wonder if some broodmares mind having to bear children year after year.

In the stall at another barn, the foal was under the watchful gaze of the nursemare, a dark bay Standardbred. When I came by, the filly was sleeping in fresh straw; her legs were stretched out, they were long and elegant, her new hooves still pristine. She looked up at me out of her sleep for a moment and then put her head back down. In Kentucky, it was another spring, another foal, and another dream for someone that might, or might not, be realized.

The Surgeon and the Colt

Dr. Larry Bramlage of Rood & Riddle moves easily between the operating room and network television, where he often provides expert commentary during racing's big events. He is one of the world's top equine orthopedic surgeons, a celebrity to horse people. With his white fringe of hair, white mustache, stocky build, and wire-rimmed glasses, he reminds me of an old-fashioned congressman popular with his constituents. Derby 2008 would find Bramlage not only explaining the death of the filly Eight Belles to the country on national television, but also performing surgery to try and save the life of an elite Thoroughbred named Chelokee who broke down at Churchill one day before the Run for the Roses.

For the racing world, the repercussions of the 2008 Kentucky Derby would linger on long after the race in months of bad press, a congressional hearing, and painful self-reflection within the sport itself, which already faced significant challenges such as declining attendance at tracks. Bramlage would play a role in the debate over racing safety by virtue of his stature and his unique insights into the fragile mechanics of the Thoroughbred racehorse.

But on the day before the Derby when Chelokee broke down,

Bramlage did not know any of that yet. He was simply doing his job at Churchill as an American Association of Equine Practitioners TV commentator. It was Kentucky Oaks day (named after the prestigious annual race for three-year-old fillies). It was rainy. The track was sloppy. The Alysheba Stakes was the eighth race. In the stretch, Chelokee was in fourth place, his eyes on home. But then he took a bad step. His right front leg gave out, and the jockey went flying. Yet the horse continued to run with the injured leg — until one of the track's outriders stopped him. Veterinarians rushed out, and the area around the horse was partitioned off with screens.

Chelokee's trainer was Michael Matz, who had also been the trainer for Barbaro. When Matz saw the colt break down, he thought, as he told me months later, "I can't believe this is happening to me now in another big race like this." He says when he rushed down to the track, vets told him Chelokee's injury appeared so severe — a major fracture — the horse should be put down.

By the time Chelokee had come to Churchill that day, he had won half of his ten starts, earning close to $400,000, and just one year before he'd won the first-ever Barbaro Stakes at Pimlico. Matz had hoped, along with the horse's owners, to take the horse all the way to the Breeders' Cup in the fall.

The horse ambulance zoomed out to the colt and took him to one of the barns (the jockey was unhurt). In an office on the backside, Dr. Foster Northrop, a longtime equine vet who often does work at Churchill Downs, had seen the breakdown on TV. He had known Chelokee for three years and loved the colt; his personality reminded him of Barbaro: gentle and agreeable. Northrop and a colleague rushed over to see Chelokee. At the barn they were told the colt had been put down. Northrop drove over to a grassy area where horses are usually euthanized. He saw Chelokee standing inside the ambulance. "He doesn't look very dead," Northrop said happily.

Northrop and Matz, who was with the colt, wanted another look at the injury. Chelokee's leg was taken out of the splint. Northrop was puzzled: No blood stained the bandage. That meant the bone had not gone through the skin. He cut the bandage off and palpated the leg: Structurally, the bones were intact. He realized after further examination that the injury was not a condylar fracture, an injury similar to Barbaro's, as had been previously thought, but an unusual fetlock (ankle joint) dislocation. The top of Chelokee's pastern was above the end of his cannon bone, not below it as it should have been. Northrop thought the horse might have a chance.

Northrop immediately radioed Bramlage and updated him. Bramlage told Northrop that he, too, thought the possibility existed that Chelokee could be saved. Matz and Chelokee's owners wanted every effort made to do so. Both veterinarians were amazed that Chelokee had not been hurt more seriously. After the injury happened, the colt was able to keep himself upright through the strength and athleticism of his supporting legs and feet. If he had fallen, the bone likely would have gone through the skin. Northrop asked Bramlage if the surgeon thought he should put the ankle back in place, if doing so would be better for the colt's blood supply. Yes, Bramlage told him.

Inside the ambulance, as another vet stabilized the horse, Northrop, with every bit of his strength, popped Chelokee's pastern back into the ankle socket. He looked up at Matz, grinned, and said, "Never done that before." But ligaments that helped bear the great weight of the horse had been destroyed and the blood supply to the injured area was in danger. Northrop wrapped the fetlock and put the horse's leg in a trauma boot. Then he bandaged the leg from the top of the boot to the knee to keep the pastern and fetlock joints from rotating, causing more damage to the soft tissue and existing nerves. The horse received an anti-inflammatory, and then the ambulance drove off, heading an hour east to Lexington and Rood

& Riddle. There, Bramlage would be his surgeon.

Chelokee's breakdown was the second time Matz and Bramlage were brought together by a horse's fate, for Bramlage had been working the 2006 broadcast of the Preakness when Barbaro broke down. Back then, Bramlage had the burden of explaining to viewers what had happened to the big bay Kentucky Derby winner. He had to do the same with Eight Belles twenty-four hours after Chelokee injured himself.

For days after Eight Belles' death, Bramlage was the equine veterinarian most in demand for comment by the *Washington Post*, *New York Times*, *Good Morning America*, and every other media outlet as had been the case after Barbaro's breakdown. Bramlage was asked not only about the medical aspects of Eight Belles' fatal injuries but whether he thought the sport should continue. He believed Eight Belles' breakdown, coupled with Barbaro's, while tragic, did not signify an epidemic and said so.

Ever since the American Association of Equine Practitioners started television's On-Call Program in 1991, in which veterinarians are on hand during broadcasts of major races and other equine events to provide expertise, Bramlage has become one of the most familiar veterinarians on the globe. (The program was formed in the aftermath of filly Go for Wand's fatal breakdown in the 1990 Breeders' Cup Distaff.) On camera, the Kansas native is concise and likeable, his Midwest roots melding nicely with the veterinarian whose research and contributions to his field have received international recognition. It seems like anyone with a horse knows who Bramlage is, especially after Barbaro's breakdown. One day at Rood & Riddle, I met two cell-phone-packing Amish horse breeders in the admissions lobby. In their straw hats, suspenders, and home-sewn clothes, they told me they were there to see Bramlage about one of their Standardbreds and had driven a few hours from Indiana to do so. It wasn't their first visit to see the vet. "He's the best in the world," said one while checking his messages. "He gets the most coverage."

Of horses, Bramlage once wrote, "The forces of nature and the hand of God created an animal as strong as an ox and as fragile as a puppy ... they are physically so well formed for athleticism and mentally so perfect for companionship that their current role for their owners is no less valuable than it was for the cavalry of the past." His love of horses comes from his parents' farm way of life and from an ex-racehorse named Buckshot his grandfather kept that Bramlage used to ride. One of my co-workers was near Bramlage when Eight Belles went down, and she saw he had tears in his eyes when he learned the filly had two broken ankles, the left fracture split through the skin. "She didn't have a front leg to stand on to be splinted and hauled off in an ambulance," Bramlage explained later in a press conference.

Although Bramlage can be genial and wisecracking with everyone from horse van drivers to owners, he is focused and intense when examining a horse and X-rays and performing surgery, and his extended silence during these procedures and others can make the people around him very nervous. But then he'll toss off a one-liner that breaks things up ... such as telling a staffer to just write "No Talent" on the top of a racehorse's chart after she could not convince clients there was no medical reason for their horse's disappointing performance. However, some clinic staff members do find Bramlage quite brusque. Whether that comes from the impatience someone of his intelligence and stature often has with the rest of us, or from the demands of his insanely busy schedule, it is difficult to say. Perhaps it is both. I don't know for certain because I didn't spend enough time with the surgeon, who is a moving target. He gives national and international presentations and has numerous commitments to professional organizations, in addition to appearing on TV, reviewing journal articles, teaching surgical residents … and don't forget his patients. He is always timing things down to the last second … like examining fifteen horses in forty minutes at five different barns located across one large farm, finishing up within an exhale to make a 10 a.m. conference call.

When Bramlage applied for a surgical residency at various schools after graduating from Kansas State's veterinary school in 1975, he was turned down for every one, a story various interns at Rood & Riddle mentioned to me, as if it gave them strength to keep pursuing their goals. Eventually, an opening showed up at Ohio State when another resident dropped out, and Bramlage ended up there, becoming a faculty member and later head of the Equine Medicine and Surgery department. He told me once if he were Gulliver (in the novel *Gulliver's Travels*) and went to the land of the Houyhnhnms

Between patients and his other commitments, Bramlage's schedule is unimaginably busy.

— a society of horses governed by reason and reason alone — "my tombstone might be, 'This guy invented the arthrodesis.' "

In his residency, Bramlage started researching how to fix fetlock injuries, the most common fatal injury in racehorses. Thoroughbreds travel at thirty-five to forty miles per hour, and "… at top speed, there is one point in every stride where [the horse's] entire weight descends upon one front leg, with most of the concussion being absorbed and dissipated by the fetlock joint," as Les Sellnow wrote in the equine health care magazine *The Horse*. For years veterinary surgeons had tried different ways to save horse's damaged ankles. When the plate was put in the front of the ankle, that didn't work because the plate didn't have any stabilization in the back. The plate would break. But when it was put in the back of the ankle, the surgical approach added to the existing problem of lost blood supply, increasing the chances of infection. That wasn't practical either.

Bramlage started to rethink things. He wanted to stay away from the primary trauma of the injury. The goal was to ensure successful wound healing and have the limb stabilized enough so the horse would be both pain-free and able to bear weight on it right away, decreasing the chances of laminitis. Horses, obviously, can't use crutches, and the weight their slender legs carry is enormous. He devised a way that surgeons could go through the front of the ankle by making an additional fracture, sawing off a sliver of the cannon bone to gain access to the joint. Then, in Bramlage's vision, a plate and screws would be put in the front, and a wire used as a tension band in the back of the ankle for stabilization. Last, the surgeon would repair the small fracture he'd made for access and exit the way he came in.

For two years, between his other responsibilities, Bramlage took his idea from theory to practice in the chilly, white-walled postmortem room, working on cadavers. In 1978, noted equine veterinarians Dr. Robert Copeland and Dr. Gary Lavin called Bramlage from

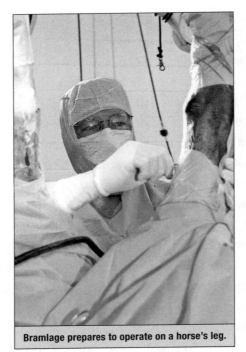

Bramlage prepares to operate on a horse's leg.

Lexington and asked if he had anything new when it came to repairing fetlock injuries. They had a mare named Melanie who had such a severe fetlock injury, she had little chance of making it without surgery. She had already developed laminitis in her opposite non-injured limb.

"I've been working on this idea, and I think it might work," Bramlage told the two vets.

Bramlage (with colleagues) fused Melanie's ankle, but she didn't make it; the laminitis was too far along. However, Bramlage was encouraged and about two years and nine fetlock fusions later (six of which had the horses back on their feet), he and another equine surgeon, Dr. William Reed, performed a fetlock arthrodesis on the colt Noble Dancer. The prominent horse was injured at Belmont Park. (Reed, now deceased, was the surgeon who operated on the doomed filly Ruffian after she broke down in the legendary 1975 match race against Kentucky Derby winner Foolish Pleasure. Ruffian injured herself coming out of anesthesia and had to be euthanized.) Noble Dancer went on to a successful stud career for more than two decades. Bramlage has now done more than 200 fetlock fusions. In 2007, the surgeon performed the procedure on another celebrity patient, Teuflesberg, the stakes-winning comet bought originally at the Target price of $9,000.

Now Teuflesberg is at stud. Today the operation is used across the country, not only for fetlock injuries but for conditions such as degenerative arthritis in joints. Its success has allowed surgeons to address more complicated injuries such as Chelokee's.

Chelokee did not undergo surgery until two days after the Derby, allowing the colt to calm down and the injured blood vessels to stabilize. In the operating room, Bramlage performed a fetlock arthrodesis on the colt, fusing his fetlock joint with a fourteen-inch-long steel plate and eighteen screws that locked into it. Cartilage was taken from his long pastern and cannon bones, which would grow together (fuse) over time, stabilized by the plate and screws, along with the wire Bramlage had inserted into the back of the ankle to replace the missing ligaments. Bramlage also replaced additional missing ligaments in the back of the pastern joint by putting in plastic cable behind that joint and through the long and short pastern bones. (Plastic was used instead of wire because it provides more flexibility for the pastern joint, which still needed to move.)

Chelokee would never race again. But he did have a chance at being a breeding stallion if he mended right. Like many surgeons, Bramlage is unflappable; he told me he felt no pressure about the surgery; he could only do his best, and it was the horse's only shot to live. But other people in the horse world told me they worried if Chelokee did not do well, the media would shine a brighter light on the story, at that point overshadowed by Eight Belles' death, and the glare would be terrible for the sport.

The day after Chelokee's surgery, Bramlage walked me over to Barn 2 to see the colt. In the stall, the sleek dark bay was formidable-looking, filling up the space with his size and presence. His muscles bulged; his eyes were intelligent and focused. He was royal. A little strip of white ran down his muzzle in the shape of an upside-down state of Florida. The bottom of his right front leg was in cast, but he looked ready to bust out and gallop back up I-64 to Churchill Downs given the chance. Chelokee was so bored in his stall he had pulled the IV line out of the ceiling for entertainment. Bramlage said the surgery had gone well and the colt was having no problems. Right now, the things to watch out for were any potential infection, making sure his blood supply stayed strong, and ensuring that the implants held up. On the left front foot he had a supportive cushioned shoe, which would stay on at all times, to help prevent laminitis.

Bramlage knew from experience that Chelokee's injury was far more difficult to recover from than a standard fetlock fracture because of the irreparable damage to the ligaments supporting the pastern joint. Without them, his healing and rehabilitation depended more on the scar tissue mending than it would for a horse with a regular break. The job of the artificial ligaments was to hold the leg in as close to the normal position as possible until scar tissue could form all around the pastern joint. (Also, horses can't go through a measured rehabilitative process like humans can, transitioning from crutches or a wheelchair.) Bramlage's recovery rate for a standard fetlock arthrodesis is over 80 percent, but with Chelokee's injury, the odds right after surgery were more like 60-40, in the colt's favor.

As Bramlage and I stood outside the stall talking and looking at the colt, Chelokee got a large erection; actually all horse erections are large. Most of the staff of Rood & Riddle and their clients were horse people, farm people, or both, and were used to such things, but I never stopped being embarrassed by them. Bramlage laughed. "Hopefully, that will be his next career," he said.

Two days post-op, Chelokee was walking and standing evenly on both feet. His temperature was normal. He hadn't gone to sleep, which Bramlage wanted to see happen so the colt would take weight off his injured leg, but other than that, everything was fine. As flight animals always on the alert for predators, horses get nervous in unfamiliar places; Chelokee was probably staying on guard, the staff surmised, especially with an injured leg that made him feel more vulnerable. Yet he didn't seem nervous or edgy: He let techs groom him and scratch his ears, and when Bramlage visited, he begged for peppermints. One day when I came by, someone had put a boom box playing soft rock outside the window of his stall. Inside the admissions building at the desk of Bramlage's assistant, Jennifer Wolery, bags of apple and oat horse treats, carrots, and peppermints spilled off her desk, sent by admirers of the horse, along with get-well cards. None of the cards had been placed inside his stall, to one tech's relief; she considered it bad luck.

***

While Chelokee healed, the media was filled with articles and op-eds discussing the questions Eight Belles' death raised about racing. Among them: Was the fact that the Derby track was dirt and not synthetic a factor? That she was a filly? What about steroid use? Trainer Richard Dutrow admitted that 2008 Derby winner Big Brown received anabolic steroids before the race (at that time, the usage was legal in Kentucky). And the biggest question: Was the industry transforming the Thoroughbred breed, creating horses that were fast and light for better returns over horses sturdier and more durable as people said existed in the past?

In June 2008, a group of Thoroughbred racing's top figures went to Washington, D.C., to testify before a congressional subcommittee about anabolic steroid use, breakdowns, and breeding. Lawmakers wanted to assess whether the industry needed federal oversight. For example, no uniform regulatory standards exist state-to-state when it comes to what medications are permitted to give a horse and how long before a race. At the hearing, racing figures were frank that the industry needed to take charge in fixing issues such as anabolic steroid use that have created a "chemical horse." As the hearing ended, however, it appeared that lawmakers wanted federal oversight, but the sinking economy in 2008-09 took higher priority and no such legislation had been introduced when this book went to press.

It is not within the scope of this book to examine in-depth the innumerable issues Eight Belles' death raised. Many factors within the past fifty years or so have contributed to changing racing from a business that was once dominated by family-owned farms dedicated to the tradition of the sport alone to one nearly everyone agrees is dominated by market forces. Those factors include syndicated racing and breeding partnerships and year-round racing.

Various articles after Eight Belles' death discussed today's market-driven trend of breeding for selling — where bloodlines are chosen first and foremost for speed and for creating a horse that looks good in the sales ring because those are the ones that fetch the highest prices, along with the fact that today's Thoroughbreds retire to stud after fewer races than in the past, before many people consider that they've proven themselves, both on the track and in terms of soundness. One such article on ESPN.com by longtime *Sports Illustrated* writer William Nack extensively quoted Kentucky Thoroughbred breeding consultant and pedigree analyst Ellen Parker. It boomeranged across the Web and argued at length about frailty in Eight Belles' bloodlines, a charge strongly denied by the pedigree consultant for Three Chimneys, the farm that bred her. The article said that beyond Eight Belles, the crisscrossing of bloodlines within family trees full of physical vulnerabilities has resulted in an outcome today where "the fastest and most popular sire lines in the world are the least durable and sound."

Bramlage has been at the forefront of racehorse safety and welfare issues since before Eight Belles' death. However, he and others do say that comparing today's Thoroughbreds to horses of the past is more complicated than it looks. In discussing durability, many people point to the fact that racehorses today run fewer starts. But part of that, according to Bramlage, can be attributed to a decline in the number of annual races (more than 6,500 fewer in 2007, for example, compared to 1997) and with trainers being more selective about which horses they run and where, since horses can now be flown to races.

Historical data to compare fatal injury rates from horses of the past to today's doesn't exist. An Associated Press survey of U.S. racetrack fatalities found over three per day in 2007, and 5,000 since 2003. Raw data from 2007 from The Jockey Club's new on-track injury reporting system found the "fatality rate of racing Thoroughbreds was 1.47 and 2.03 per 1,000 starts on synthetic surface and dirt, respectively," according to Dr. Mary Scollay, the vet who collected it. Statistics scheduled for release in 2009 will contain epidemiological analysis the 2007 stats did not, as well as data from far more tracks. Scollay cautions that it's too early to conclude synthetic surfaces are statistically safer due to factors such as regulatory presence, jockey caliber, and above all, human judgment: how trainers, owners, and vets treat and make decisions about their horses, something she says has not been discussed nearly enough in the entire debate about racing safety. ("We are aware of individuals who have higher [injury] rates than other individuals," yet the horses are coming from the relatively same gene pool, Scollay says. "... To me, the human factor is something that has just been overlooked.") In addition to research previously mentioned in this book being done with MRI and biomarkers to predict and prevent breakdowns, other research includes heart rate variability analysis and the use of sound waves to detect microcracks in bones that could lead to fractures.

Meanwhile, in a report to The Jockey Club at its 2008 Round Table Conference, Bramlage, a member of its Thoroughbred Safety

Committee, said, among other findings, data shows that Thorough-breds that begin racing as two-year-olds show "less predisposition to injury than horses that did not begin racing until their three-year-old year," with longer, more successful careers. This contradicts much of the popular belief that horses have to mature to a certain point before they can be put into race training. "These data strongly support the physiologic premise that it is easier for a horse to adapt to training when training begins at the end of skeletal growth," he said. When I asked him to explain further, he said, "Growth requires cells and blood supply. Adaptation to training requires cells and a blood supply. Growth stops at two years old. If you don't train by that time, that support system goes away since growth has stopped. If you then start training (later) you have to recreate it, which takes time and makes it harder for the horse to adapt to training."

As far as Eight Belles, her death brought some key changes to

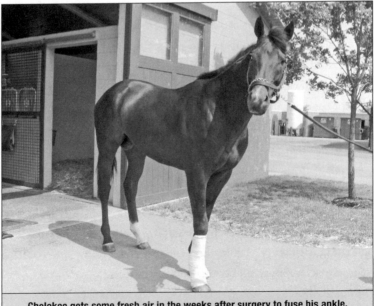

Chelokee gets some fresh air in the weeks after surgery to fuse his ankle.

racing, including more states banning anabolic steroids and safety reforms across the board at major racetracks based on Jockey Club recommendations. For some people, the changes are significant; for others they are too little, too late. More changes may come. Many horse people I talked to want a new paradigm in racing, where helping to care for a racehorse's retirement is seen as part of the responsibility of owning one, and where the industry takes a role in ensuring that the animals aren't tossed out like Styrofoam cups when they're no longer useful. In early 2009 the American Association of Equine Practitioners addressed the retirement issue when the group released a white paper recommending major changes to the sport, among them: "the development in all racing jurisdictions of a program for rehabilitation, retraining, and adoption for horses whose racing careers have ended," as well as industry-generated funds to help the horses move into second careers.

***

A second career as a stud looked like a good possibility for Chelokee in the weeks after his operation with his recovery going relatively smoothly. He also seemed to be enjoying himself as the most popular horse at the hospital. He was good-looking and knew it, smart, proud, and a little goofy. A four-year-old horse is at the end of the puppyhood stage of equine maturity, and Chelokee loved playing with the red and green balls someone had put inside his stall and pulling on people's clothes. Sometimes, the way women around Rood & Riddle talked about Chelokee reminded me of the way girls discuss boys in high school.

"He's a jock (said admiringly). But it seems like all he cares about is himself."

"He's just so handsome."

"He's like a little boy. He'll mess around with you, pretend he's going to try and be bad, but he doesn't have a mean bone in his body."

After the colt had his first cast change two weeks after the operation, his coronary band, the circle of vascular tissue whose critical job it is to nurture and grow the hoof wall, was healthy, undamaged by the period of lost blood supply. His entire foot looked good, his incisions healed. No soft areas were evident that might have indicated infection. The horse had lost skin on the back of his ankle due to the vascular damage, but nothing serious or deep into the tissue, and healthy tissue was underneath the areas that had sloughed off. The vet's plan was to leave the cast off for a couple of days and let the tendons move and stretch. Doing so would make the colt's transition to bearing weight easier. The next cast would leave his toe open, allowing for a little bit of motion in the tendon as he stepped, creating another transitional stage. The radiographs of the injured fetlock showed no problems. Just as important, the X-rays of the supporting limbs also showed laminitis had not begun.

About one month after the operation, it was time for that open-toe cast to come off, "the last critical transition," according to Bramlage. From here on out, the colt would wear only a bandage for support. It was an early June day, steaming hot. When I got to the hospital, Chelokee was already in a radiology room. His dark mane was parted down the middle, his gaze confident. He was the equine version of homecoming king.

Bramlage was in his trademark Smurf-blue scrubs. The small cast saw he held in his hands had a blade on the end that looked like a pizza cutter. He turned it on and began to roll it back and forth over the purple cast on the horse's right front leg. Dust flaked off into a little purple pile. Chelokee, the sedation having now taken effect, hung his head.

Sheri Miller, one of Bramlage's techs, held two sets of cast spreaders in her hand, one small, one large; they looked a little like pliers. She handed the small set to Bramlage first, and he pried the cast

During his long stay at the hospital, Chelokee, shown here with tech Dana Kielar, was one of the most popular horses, charming the staff with his regal bearing and playfulness.

open. Chelokee's lips quivered, his eyes were downcast. Another tech gently held his ears.

"Pick him up," Bramlage said to Miller, and she lifted his right front hoof. "The big one now," he said, and Miller handed him the large set of cast spreaders. Then to Chelokee, "We'll get this off you in a minute."

Bramlage pried the cast completely off. A funky smell filled the room, gym-locker-like. Bits of moist hay were stuck to his hoof. A translucent protective patch designed to keep the cast from rubbing the skin was stuck to the leg. It was red from the scarlet oil, an antibacterial ointment applied to the wound to help facilitate the healing. Bramlage peeled the patch back to show the damp, sticky skin.

"As soon as we get some X-rays, let's sweat him," Bramlage said, referring to a process done to take down the swelling in the soft tissue. An ointment is applied to the fetlock and then it is wrapped in plastic with another bandage on top of that.

After the X-rays were taken, Bramlage put them on the light stand. I gathered with the techs and several interns around him. He looked at them without saying anything for what seemed like forever. The vet's face was unreadable. Sweat rolled down his left temple.

"He's got a little pastern sag," Bramlage said finally. The pastern joint was bending backward slightly, caused by both the original ligamentous injury and the fact that the pastern was now being asked to do some of the job of the fetlock. Then the veterinarian kept looking at the films.

Finally, Bramlage said, "So far, so good." Dr. Megan Romano, an intern, put a final set of X-rays on the screen, and he said, "That's great." The implants were "solid" and the bone fusing. The healing was on track. The supporting limb showed no signs of problems. Everyone around Bramlage exhaled. With the cast now off, the test in the coming weeks would be how the pastern joint took the added weight load, and how the (natural) ligaments and tendons moved and adjusted to life without a movable fetlock joint.

Throughout the summer Chelokee held court in Barn 2, continuing to charm the staff. The colt was a ham. When journalists came to see him, he posed for photographers, making sure they got his best side. Unlike some other horses, he loved his baths. He didn't squirm or try and get away. As the stream from the hose hit him, he became motionless, reveling in the feel of the water against his coat.

In late summer, as his exercise load was being increased to thirty-minute walks twice a day, the colt started to get sore on his left front leg. He was stretching his pastern joint in the injured right front, which put more weight on the opposing limb. It was worrisome. Laminitis could develop. In discussing the fetlock arthrodesis, Miller, one of Bramlage's techs, once said: "It can make you feel like you've done the best thing in the entire world, or it will break your heart."

To deal with Chelokee's sore limb, Bramlage changed his medication and altered his exercise. Eventually, the colt came around. By the end of August he was ready to go to Vinery, a stud farm in Lexington, for further recuperation and, fingers crossed, a stud career.

The day Chelokee left for Vinery, he got a bath. After that, he was groomed and fussed over by the techs and barn crew. When the trailer came to pick him up, he walked steadily toward it. Right before he stepped up, he stopped, looked around a moment (for the cameras?) and boarded. A prince was healthy again.

Bramlage would continue to visit Chelokee on the farm, monitoring his progress. The colt and other Bluegrass Thoroughbreds are, as someone put it to me at a party, the only patients left in the state who still get house calls by their doctors.

***

Every dream for a Derby winner begins in the breeding shed. Bramlage says a new stallion is similar to a new NFL running back. "They have three years to prove their worth," he said, referring to how important it is for them to produce effective athletes at the track and that their three-year-old sons and daughters are the first and most important test. Despite some big names, stallions can come and go like reality show stars. The most heart-wrenching story I know about a failed stallion is that of Ferdinand. The gentle, chestnut 1986 Derby winner was unsuccessful as a stud in the United States and ended up in Japan in 1994 where, also a disappointment in the breeding shed after several years, he was eventually sold to a slaughterhouse and most likely turned into pet food.

Chelokee came from solid sire Cherokee Run, whose offspring include Zanjero, War Pass, and Chilukki, each with lifetime earnings of over $1 million. But he had never won a grade I race like the Breeders' Cup, which is what top breeders want. He had to contend with the press surrounding his injury. Plus, in 2009 when he went to stud, the economy was in trouble, and the horse industry reflected it, with most farms reducing their stud fees. The first week of January 2009, Vinery had its stallion open house. Thoroughbred mares start being bred every year in mid-February, and the yearly open house is a parade of studs for horse people out matchmaking for their mares, and for the media and fans.

Chelokee had been doing well since he left Rood & Riddle at summer's end. But four days before the open house he started having problems traveling correctly on his right front foot, the same leg on which he'd had the arthrodesis. It turned out the horse had bruised the soft tissue of his right front heel. Dr. Vern Dryden of Rood & Riddle's podiatry department rushed over to see what could be done. Chelokee's bruised heel was soaked in Epsom salts and wrapped in a bran mash poultice. Dryden shod him the next day with a specialized shoe. "The way he travels causes him to load that heel very hard," Dryden told me. "He doesn't have the flexibility because his fetlock is fused. ..." The horse was still adapting to his new anatomy. His size and the severity of his injury made it more difficult than it would be for most horses.

The day of the open house was cold with occasional puffs of snow, some liquid sun. At Vinery, the scene reminded me of the red carpet at a Hollywood movie premiere. Inside the farm's huge white clapboard barn topped by spires, the horses were groomed and lustrous. Crowds of people stood at the entrance as a man in a green Vinery jacket called a stallion's name ... "RePENT!" and another green-jacketed handler escorted the stud up to the onlookers, stopping underneath the square of light filtering through the cupola above. Cameras flashed as the stud's bloodlines were recited.

In an adjacent barn, at tables covered with white tablecloths, people nibbled on cheese sandwiches and drank wine as they leafed

Chelokee overcame the odds to join the stallion roster at Vinery farm.

through the glossy stallion catalog. A flat-screen TV flanked by ever-green trees replayed the different stallions' races.

Back inside the stallion barn, Chelokee was in his stall. He wasn't being led out because of his foot. Nobody in the crowd asked why; spectators would just gather around his stall periodically, and a Vinery worker would open the door so they could get a look. When I was there, Chelokee came up to the entrance of his stall and gave everyone photo-ops and then circled around the space with no problems walking at all. He looked healthy, handsome, and energetic. He bucked his back legs up occasionally.

"He's got a pretty eye," said one woman watching him, as her friend took pictures. After a while, the crowd left and the stall door closed. But Chelokee was fired up; he began bucking around again. Across the way, a barn worker said, "He's not as laid-back as his dad, but part of it is being cooped up." Then Chelokee kicked the stall with his back legs, on purpose. Maybe for the hell of it or to let someone know he wanted to get out in the paddock. The sound made me shudder, knowing the bill for his front leg had cost at least twice the down payment on my house. But Chelokee is a horse, not a person, who, after having a catastrophic injury one year earlier, would probably have still been cautious with how he threw his body around. Horses don't look back. For Chelokee's part, his health crisis was over. By the beginning of spring he had covered (bred) twenty mares, not as many as 2007 Breeders' Cup Dirt Mile winner Corinthian across town (managed by the same partnership) who had covered 100 mares and counting, but a good showing in a bad economy for a horse in his circumstances. Now Chelokee's three-year clock had begun ticking.

Chelokee is one of hundreds of horses that have been saved by Bramlage's development of the fetlock arthrodesis. People often want to know from Bramlage, as well as the other vets at Rood & Riddle, "Why do some horses recover from catastrophic injuries and others don't?"

Bramlage's reply when he was a guest on the Webcast "Talkin' Horses" was: "There is no answer to this question. It is like asking why some car accident victims survive and some don't. It is the sum total of the various aspects of very complex injuries, the response of the horse, both in healing and in caring for themselves, and a certain degree of luck that determines the outcome."

In other words, equine veterinarians can't play God any more than human physicians can. Why one patient with the same injury heals over another is, like a horse's mind, unfathomable.

Afterword

During my year at Rood & Riddle I learned one truth from observing the vets, clients, and horses: You can do everything right when it comes to any kind of horse, and things can still go to hell in a handbasket over something as small as an unfilled hole in the ground, as inconsequential as a bad step, as uncontrollable as a mayfly carrying Potomac Horse Fever. People who own horses know this, and yet they want to own them nevertheless. When I asked why, they talked about the pure, indescribable bond of equine friendship, and how taking care of horses ties them to a way of life that follows the seasons, in accord with the sun and the moon, and the cycles of birth and death. Those in the racing world — owners, breeders, and trainers — said things like, "Once it gets in your blood, it's there forever. Win or lose. I don't know why." Or, "You only invest what you can afford to lose. Anyway, what isn't a risk? Life's a gamble whatever you do."

Throughout the year I saw that people need horses more than horses need people, whether it is an owner with the dream of the winner's circle on Derby Day or someone with an illness or life setback who finds strength and determination through the love of a horse or the example of its courage. I came to see horses save people more than the other way around.

Since 1986 when the clinic opened, it has grown right up the boundaries of the land Man o' War ran around as a foal. But the Thoroughbred industry that currently provides the majority of its clients faces challenges apart from the tragedy of the 2008 Derby. For starters, there's development. Since around 1990, a building boom in the Lexington region has eaten up acres of farmland. (In 2006 the World Monuments Fund named the Bluegrass landscape one of the most distinctive on the globe and one of the most endangered.) Efforts such as a local government program to purchase development rights to protect farmland have been enacted to try to curb some of the subdivisions, strip malls, and other building. In tandem, the racing industry is searching for ways to stay viable and relevant in a new century. At this writing the Kentucky legislature is looking at allowing slot machines at the tracks, as other states are doing, in an attempt to increase purse size and attendance. Those against the slots say it will increase crime and gambling. Proponents say it is essential to stay competitive and save the thousands of jobs in the Bluegrass that depend on the Thoroughbred business. Dr. Bill Rood tells me he doesn't worry; he believes horse farms will always be in the Bluegrass and that the sport and show horse community is growing in the area, especially with the expansion of the Kentucky Horse Park. Dr. Tom Riddle feels the same way. But other people do worry, like the various Thoroughbred farm managers and barn crew I met throughout the year. But whatever happens in the future, right now across the Bluegrass plenty of horses graze in the paddocks and shift in the stalls; stallions and mares breed, and foals turn and grow and dream inside their mothers, dreaming whatever it is foals dream about. Inside all of that, a herd of veterinarians and staff at Rood & Riddle is up early, ready to take care of them.

Notes on Reporting

Prologue: "Once I asked Riddle if writer E.B. White's advice ..." *Here Is New York*, by E.B. White (The Little Bookroom, 2000; 3rd printing).

2. Although the vast majority of animals in Eight Belles' situation are euthanized immediately, at least one vet, Dr. R.F. Redden of Versailles, Kentucky, does not agree with many colleagues that they should be. In a May 11, 2008, article in the *Lexington Herald-Leader*, Redden argued that emergency protocol when it comes to catastrophic injuries at racetracks should be changed. He said in his experience even horses with open fractures are not necessarily suffering so greatly that they need to be euthanized immediately, nor does he believe they cannot be saved. Redden said they should be managed in such a way — with splints, for example, and then transported to a hospital — to give everyone involved time to think carefully about the medical options.

Chapter 1, Hello Weekend: "... broodmare wombs are 'miniature economies.' " I have borrowed a phrase from Bill Farish, head of Lane's End horse farm, quoted in a February 21, 2009, article ("Not all is gloomy in breeding shed") in the *Lexington Herald-Leader* by Alicia Wincze. Farish was referring to sires but I think it applies to broodmares, too: "Each stallion is like their own little mini economy."

Chapter 2, Enigmas: "For instance, when Catherine the Great traveled ..." *The Great Upheaval: America and the Birth of the Modern World 1788-1800,* by Jay Winik (Harper, 2007).

2. "In China, one of the fathers of equine acupuncture ..." I read about Sun Yang in numerous sources including the 1996 book *Veterinary Medicine: An Illustrated History,* by Robert H. Dunlop and David J. Williams (Mosby, 1996). This is also the source for my reference to equine medicine being an extremely respected career at the time of Sun's life.

3. "The roots of Chinese medicine are in the science of Taoism. ..." Reprinted courtesy of the International Veterinary Acupuncture Society.

4. "I can't show you the million-dollar barn, ..." May 3, 1997, *Lexington Herald-Leader* article, "Breeding Ground for Royalty," by Maryjean Wall.

Chapter 3, Thrilling: Information about Stanley Dancer is from September 9, 2005, *New York Times* obituary.

2. Description of Valley Victory bowing out of the Hambletonian is from August 2, 1989, *New York Times* article: "An Illness Forces Valley Victory to Pass Up Hambletonian," by Alex Yannis.

3. "That horse was so full of himself." From August 6, 2007, article on Harnesslink.com, "Hambletonian Winner Defies Jinx." At the Link (blog) with Carol Hodes.

4. Description of Valley Victory offspring's temperament is from undated article "Valley Victory: The Sire of the '90s" by Kimberly A. Rinker on oddsonracing.com.

Chapter 4, Repro Cowboys: "Once, according to a news story ..." January 23, 1989, article in the *Lexington Herald-Leader* by Jacqueline Duke about Claiborne vet Dr. Walter Kaufman.

2. Statistics on foaling months of Kentucky Derby come courtesy of turf writer and handicapper Dick Downey.

Chapter 5, Divine Mare: "... in summer 2008, a group of camels, llamas, zebras, and swine escaped ..." June 20, 2008, Reuters article: "Dutch police suspect giraffe for circus breakout."

2. "... the dogs of an older woman trapped for 196 hours following a huge earthquake ..." June 28, 2008, Associated Press article: "Rare shelter in China takes canine earthquake survivors."

3. "Horse personality: Variation between breeds." August 2008, *Applied Animal Behavior Science*, Vol. 112, Issues 3-4. Adele Sian Lloyd, Joanne Elizabeth Martin, Hannah Louise Imogen, Bornett Gauci, and Robert George Wilkinson.

4. "Personality differences and individual differences in the horse, their significance, use, and measurement." 1998 *Equine Clinical Behavior* article by D.S. Mills, De Montfort University, U.K.

5. Animal communicator who "interviewed" John Henry was Nancy Regalmuto, May 1985 *Equus* article: "Special report: The Anatomy of a Winner."

Chapter 7, Vet-School Hot: "A 2007 Australian study of veterinarians ..." July 2007, *Australian Veterinary Journal*, "Longitudinal study of veterinary students and veterinarians: family and gender issues after 20 years." Volume 85, Issue 7.

Chapter 8, Piaff: "Routes are not all precise ..." *Within Reach: My Everest Story,* by Mark Pfetzer and Jack Galvin. (Dutton, 1998). Reprinted with permission.

2. "It said the French call their dogs bêtes de chagrin ..." September/October 2007 issue of *Orion*: "What's the Use of Pets?" by Ginger Strand.

3. "It was like a color was missing from her life." Personal interview with veterinarian and veterinary scholar Myrna Milani, March 2008.

Chapter 10, Lucky: Eight Belles' memorial service reconstructed from YouTube videos from the Kentucky Derby Museum and August 6, 2008, article in *Lexington Herald-Leader* by Amy Wilson: "Filly gave all in run for the roses."

Chapter 12, Steps: "… blizzards in Colorado in 1949 and 1950 that resulted in numerous range bulls getting frost-bitten scrotums …" From 1996 book *Veterinary Medicine: An Illustrated History*, by Robert H. Dunlop and David J. Williams (Mosby, 1996).

2. "In 1924, a young German surgical resident, defying his boss' orders, performed the first human heart catheterization …" Referring to Werner Forssmann, described in *Veterinary Medicine* mentioned above, as well as in humorous detail in *Mavericks, Miracles, and Medicine: The pioneers who risked their lives to bring medicine into the Modern Age* by Julie M. Fenster (Carroll & Graf, 2003).

Chapter 13, Surely Awesome: "A good jockey is part-horse …" Attributed to Drew Mollica, agent of late winning jockey Chris Antley, read in *Two Minutes to Glory: The Official History of the Kentucky Derby* by Pamela K. Brodowsky and Tom Philbin, in cooperation with Churchill Downs (HarperCollins, 2007).

2. "In one account of Greek mythology …" From *Mythology* by Edith Hamilton (Little, Brown, and Company, 1942).

Chapter 14, Worries: Information about Calumet Farm comes from *Wild Ride: The Rise and Fall of Calumet Farm Inc., America's Premier Racing Dynasty* (Henry Holt, 1994), by Ann Hagedorn Auerbach.

Chapter 15, The Surgeon and the Colt: Description of Chelokee's breakdown drawn from interviews with Drs. Foster Northrop and Larry Bramlage, as well as trainer Michael Matz. However, Brendan O'Meara's January 3, 2009, story in *The Blood-Horse*, "Life Beyond Racing," was extremely helpful for background.

2. "Of horses, Bramlage once wrote ..." Introduction to *The Horse Doctors*, an overview of the American Association of Equine Practitioners (David Stoecklein & Stoecklein Publishing, 2004).

3. Although the information on arthrodesis comes from personal interviews with Bramlage, the August 1, 2008, article "Fetlock arthrodesis boost survival rates," by Ed Kane, PhD, in *DVM Newsmagazine*, was another very helpful resource for background.

4. "One such article on ESPN.com ..." William Nack article on May 16, 2008, entitled "Eight Belles' breakdown, a predictable tragedy."

5. "(Bramlage) and others say comparing today's Thoroughbreds ..." Resources include the July 1, 2008, article in *The Horse* by Stacey Oke, DVM, MSc, "Understanding and Preventing Catastrophic Injuries," as well as the transcript from The Jockey Club's 56th annual Roundtable Conference.

Many other books were read in the course of researching *Equine ER*. Some of the most valuable include:

All Creatures Great and Small by James Herriot (St Martin's Griffin, 2004).

A Short History of Veterinary Medicine in America by B.W. Bierer (Michigan State University Press, 1955).

Barbaro: The Horse Who Captured America's Heart by Sean Clancy (Eclipse Press, 2007).

Chosen by a Horse: A Memoir by Susan Richards (Soho, 2006).

Color Atlas of the Horse's Foot by Christopher C. Pollitt, BVSc, PhD (Mosby-Wolfe, 1995).

Complications: A Surgeon's Notes on an Imperfect Science by Atul Gawande (Metropolitan Books, 2002).

From Foal to Champion, Photographs by Dell Hancock, text by Edward L. Bowen (Stewart, Tabori & Chang, 1991).

Hoofbeats and Society: Studies of Human-Horse Interactions by Elizabeth Atwood Lawrence (Indiana University Press, 1985).

Horse Owner's Veterinary Handbook, 2nd Edition, by James M. Giffin M.D., and Tom Gore, DVM. (Howell Book House, 1989).

Horse Sense for People by Monty Roberts (Penguin, 2002).

Manual of Equine Emergencies, Treatment & Procedures by James A. Orsini, DVM, Diplomate ACVS and Thomas J. Divers, DVM, Diplomate ACVIM, AVECC. (W.B. Saunders Company, 1998).

She Flies Without Wings: How Horses Touch a Woman's Soul by Mary D. Midkiff (Delta, 2002).

Stud: Adventures in Breeding by Kevin Conley (Bloomsbury, 2002).

The Complete Equine Veterinary Manual by Tony & Marcy Pavord (David & Charles, 1997).

The Horse Behaviour Handbook by Abigal Hogg (David & Charles, 2003).

The Horse's Health Care Bible by Colin Vogel (David & Charles, 2002).

The Soul of a Horse by Joe Camp (Three Rivers Press, 2009).

Understanding Equine Colic by Bradford G. Bentz, VMD, MS. (Blood-Horse Publications, 2004).

Understanding Horse Behavior by Lesley Skipper. (Skyhorse, 2007).

Understanding the Equine Foot by Fran Jurga (Blood-Horse Publications, 1998).

Acknowledgments

This book is for my mother, Estelle Hamburg, with love and gratitude. Thank you to Jacqueline Duke, editor of Eclipse Press, for the terrific editing, and for all the ideas, input, and support, and to Drs. Bill Rood and Tom Riddle and all the veterinarians, clients, horses, horse people, and Rood & Riddle staff members who contributed. Heartfelt thanks to Billie Brownell for contacting me about this project and playing an instrumental role in its inception. Other thanks: Robin Murray, the clinic's head of P.R., and the administrative assistants for the vets, present and past: Heather Dunaway, Kaye Kincaid, Natalie King, Jackie Landis, Whitney Mathes, Elizabeth McCutcheon, Dee Shuping, Julia Vassar, Sarah Weed, and Jen Wolery, and barn manager Erin Mathes. Also: Alexandra Beckstett and Jennifer Haas Hoyt at Eclipse Press; Dan Liebman at *The Blood-Horse*; writers Jon Katz and Susan Richards; Dr. Bryan Waldridge; Chad Mendell; the Author's Guild; and Katherine Olney.

Thanks to my dear friend Mary Gay Broderick and, also, for their support and friendship: Sandra Moody-Ayers, Dan Fost, Tom Meyer, Jessalyn Nash, Kevin Smokler; Peter and Pat Sussman; Rosie Moosnick; along with Jerry, Steve, Jenny, Riley, Rosie, Ethan, and Daisy Guttman. Eternal gratitude to Trice Bonney, Linda Chrisman, Christine Ciavarella, Sarah Dandridge, Michael Ratener, and Elizabeth Padron Vos.

Photo Credits

About the Author

L eslie Guttman was born in upstate New York, into a family with a love of books and of the public library, and grew up in Lexington, Kentucky. She received a degree in journalism from Indiana University at Bloomington and also studied at the University of Califor-

nia at Berkeley. She worked at the *San Francisco Chronicle* for more than fifteen years, as both an editor and writer. Leslie's work also has appeared in such publications as the *Washington Post*, *Salon*, and *Orion*. In addition, Leslie has worked at *Wired* magazine, and her public radio commentary has been broadcast on KQED-FM in San Francisco and nationally on "Marketplace."

Her awards include being honored by the Society of Professional Journalists for outstanding journalism, as well as a "Salute to Excellence" award by the National Association of Black Journalists. She has guest-lectured at college journalism programs in both San Francisco and the Bluegrass.

Leslie currently lives in Lexington. *Equine ER* is her first book.

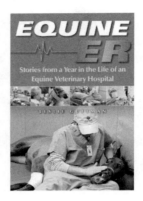

The writing and reporting of *Equine ER* was documented through a video series, as well as photos and blog posts, available on **http://www.equineer.blogspot.com**. Some of the stories in this book, such as the journey of Ten Hail Marys (Chapter 5: Divine Mare) are featured on the site, as well as others. The site also gives a window into such arenas as the clinic's intensive care unit during foaling season.